MOUNTAIN WALKING
IN SOUTHERN CATALUNYA

About the Authors

After leaving their academic careers in 2002, Philip and Vivien Freakley moved to the Haute Ariege region of the French Pyrenees to indulge a lifelong passion for mountains and the natural world. They are, by inclination, fair weather walkers and discovered the mountains of Southern Catalunya during an escape from a particularly cold and snowy Pyrenean winter. Their first explorations were prompted by curiosity – as to why none of the English language guidebooks gives the region more than a passing mention. This is still something of a mystery. In 2004 the authors bought a house here and have spent the subsequent five winters exploring, talking to local walkers, researching local route descriptions, knitting together apparently unrelated scraps of footpath and encouraging everyone to build cairns. Now they are looking forward to the company of more English-speaking walkers in these surprising mountains.

MOUNTAIN WALKING
IN SOUTHERN CATALUNYA

by
Philip and Vivien Freakley

2 POLICE SQUARE, MILNTHORPE, CUMBRIA LA7 7PY
www.cicerone.co.uk

Printed by KHL Printing, Singapore

A catalogue record for this book is available from the British Library.
All photographs are by the authors unless otherwise stated.

Acknowledgements

Firstly, our thanks go to Elies Bel Mestres, neighbour and els Ports enthusiast, for suggesting the idea of an English language guide and for much subsequent information and assistance.

The walks described in this guide owe much to the work of the members of the Unió de Excursionista de Catalunya (UEC) de Tortosa, who developed and waymarked the network of footpaths. The benefits for the authors have been two-fold, firstly to give us the confidence to venture into some very steep and complicated terrain and, secondly, to assist us in describing the routes. Our exploration of els Ports has also been substantially aided by the route descriptions (in Catalan) of Joan Tirón Ferré. His generosity in welcoming an English guidebook to join his several guidebooks of the area is very much appreciated.

Margaret Laird and Robert Weller have given much of their time to walking the routes and checking the descriptions and their comments have been immensely valuable in helping to shape the final text. The support of Eva Cid Aranda has been of substantial value throughout, and particularly for introducing two key people: Roberto Asensio, who proposed Walk 2 and explained the complicated rules and regulations of hunting; and Salomé Aguilar, who helped with information and translation. The assistance of several organisations is also acknowledged: the Observatori de l'Ebre, for compiling long-term weather data; the Patronat de Turisme de la Diputació de Tarragona, for a wealth of information, advice and assistance, provided by Silvia Forcadell Rodriguez; and the Parc Natural dels Ports organisation for helpful discussions.

Front cover: The window of la Foradada on the Serra de Montsia ridge (Walk 29)

CONTENTS

Advice to Readers

Readers are advised that, while every effort is made by our authors to ensure the accuracy of guidebooks as they go to print, changes can occur during the lifetime of an edition. Please check Updates on this book's page on the Cicerone website (www.cicerone.co.uk) before planning your trip. We would also advise that you check information about such things as transport, accommodation and shops locally. Even rights of way can be altered over time. We are always grateful for information about any discrepancies between a guidebook and the facts on the ground, sent by email to info@cicerone.co.uk or by post to Cicerone, 2 Police Square, Milnthorpe LA7 7PY, United Kingdom.

Map Key

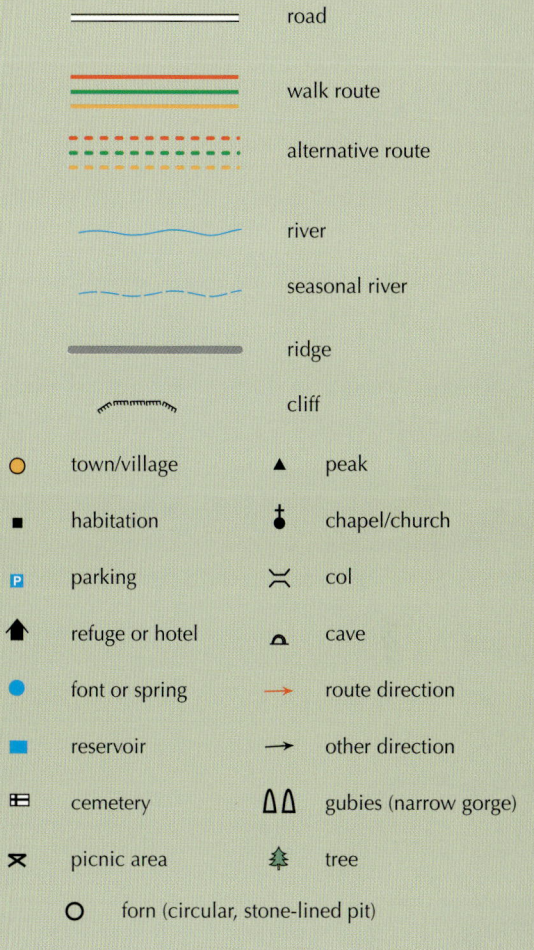

	road		
	walk route		
	alternative route		
	river		
	seasonal river		
	ridge		
	cliff		
○	town/village	▲	peak
■	habitation	♁	chapel/church
P	parking	≍	col
⬆	refuge or hotel	⌂	cave
●	font or spring	→	route direction
◼	reservoir	→	other direction
⊞	cemetery	△△	gubies (narrow gorge)
✕	picnic area	🌲	tree
○	forn (circular, stone-lined pit)		

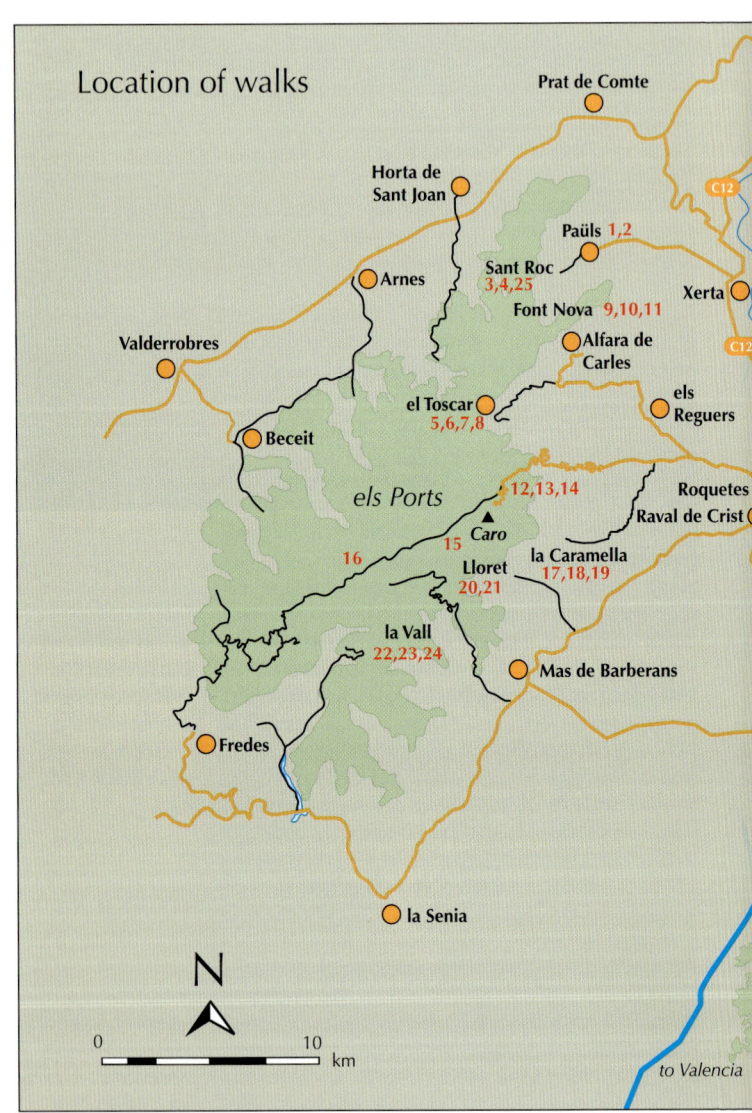

Location of walks

Prat de Comte

C12

Horta de
Sant Joan

Paüls 1,2

Sant Roc
3,4,25

Xerta

Arnes

Font Nova 9,10,11

Valderrobres

Alfara de
Carles

C12

els
Reguers

el Toscar
5,6,7,8

Beceit

els Ports

12,13,14

Roquetes

Caro

Raval de Crist

16

15

la Caramella
17,18,19

Lloret
20,21

la Vall
22,23,24

Mas de Barberans

Fredes

N

la Senia

0   10 km

to Valencia

Some 40mins from the start of the walk up Mola Castellona the path ascends a rocky slope (Walk 19)

INTRODUCTION

Between the Coll d'Atans and the Coll de la Gilaberta (Walk 1)

It is rare to stumble across an easily accessible coastal mountain region which is practically unknown beyond its immediate boundaries. Even more so when it is discovered to have well developed walking and climbing routes. Southern Catalunya may be unique in this respect. Moreover, it is an area of remarkable natural beauty and diversity. The immense limestone crags, ridges and pinnacles of the Parc Natural dels Ports overlook the broad orange and olive tree-clad river plain of the River Ebro (Ebre in Catalan), giving a high drama to the landscape. Downstream the river flows out to the Mediterranean through the Parc Natural del Delta de l'Ebre, where salt- and freshwater lagoons support thousands of visiting, migrating and resident birds.

The region has not been much visited by walkers from the UK, perhaps because it is not obvious from the general tourist maps and guides that it even has significant mountains. In fact, with its benign winter climate, it has a great deal to offer walkers from October through to May. This is well appreciated by the members of the local section of the Catalan walking and climbing club, who are very enthusiastic and active and, naturally, proud of their region. They have

Pathless territory on the way to the summit of Moleta de les Canals (Walk 3)

waymarked networks of old paths and trails, as well as pioneering some new routes, to enable walkers to experience even the remoter parts. Even so, in comparison with other developed walking areas, the number of people out on the hills is very, very low. In fact, outside weekends and holidays, it is rare to encounter anyone other than the occasional goatherd. Walkers from outside the region are welcomed for a very pragmatic reason – the footpaths need traffic to keep them open.

THE WALKING AREA

This relatively unknown walking area is in Tarragona, the most southerly province of Catalunya. It includes the highest part of an extensive mountain region that extends over the border into the province of Valencia to the south and up to the city of Tarragona in the north. This guide describes walks in three mountain groups rising from the plain of the River Ebre: the els Ports massif to the west, the Serra de Cardó to the east and the Serra de Montsia to the south-east. The small medieval city of Tortosa, straddling the river, affords good access to all three groups. It is approximately 180km south of Barcelona and 200km north of Valencia. In addition, the local section of the long-distance coastal path is included. The Location of Walks map shows the situation of Tortosa in relation to the mountain groups, as well as showing the starting points of the walks.

Most of the routes in this guide-book are in the els Ports massif, which rises abruptly from sea level to the highest point of 1442m at Mont Caro. It comprises a complex network of narrow valleys and extensive ridges over 1100m, bounded by spectacular cliffs on its eastern side. The lower slopes of the Parc Natural are a jumble of wooded valleys and terraced *fincas* (country estates), over-looked by steep cliffs and fantastic pinnacles. The paths find their way up, down and around some apparently impossible slopes onto the main massif, where the views are extensive and dramatic. There are surprises at every turn. The nature of the terrain is extremely diverse, often passing from stark karst features to dense pine and holly oak woodland within a few hundred metres of walking, but with a pleasingly low proportion of the thorny scrub which characterises most Mediterranean walking.

The Serra de Cardó offers a landscape of forested slopes, dramatic limestone escarpments and ruined chapels perched on rocky crags. Water is plentiful here from many springs, and the air is uncharacteristically soft for the Mediterranean. The Serra de Montsia forms a high ridge with diverse vegetation, from fragrant herbage on open hillsides to dense shade in valleys lined with holm oaks. Being close to the sea, the views over the Delta and along the coast are exceptional. On a clear day it is possible to see as far north as Tarragona. In sharp contrast to the three mountain groups, the coastal path between

The coastal path weaves between coves, cliffs and olive groves (Walk 30)

the small towns of l'Ampolla and l'Ametlla de Mar winds its way over low cliffs, passing numerous small coves and pebbly beaches. The clarity of the water here is superb, although rather cool for swimming during the winter months. The Montsia and the coastal path provide sheltered walks when there are strong north-west winds on the high ridges of els Ports.

The variety and nature of the terrain is largely a result of it being sculpted primarily by wind and water. Glacial action, which produces larger and simpler landforms, did not reach this far south. Consequently, it has been possible to propose a diversity of routes within a relatively small geographical area. Typical driving times from Tortosa are in the region of 30–45 minutes.

THE NATURAL PARKS

The Parc Natural dels Ports was founded in June 2001, increasing the protection for the environment and wildlife offered by its previous designation as a Reserva Nacional de Caça (national hunting reserve). It covers 35,050 hectares where the regions of Catalunya, Aragon and Valencia converge and has 867 hectares of special nature reserve, largely dedicated to a protected area of ancient forest. The name 'els Ports' can be translated as 'the gateways' (into the mountains). The region has been inhabited since prehistoric times and exploited throughout the centuries for its timber.

Traces of subsistence farming and resource exploitation are found throughout the Parc in the form of ruined farm buildings, animal

The Mas de la Roca
in the Vallcervera

shelters, drystone terrace walls, lime-kilns, tar pits, charcoal burning clearings, irrigation channels and protected water sources. However, apart from some cattle farming (breeding of bulls), sheep pasturing and olive, almond and cherry orchards, there is little agriculture nowadays. The Parc is now a haven for wildlife and walkers.

The other natural park of the region, the Delta de l'Ebre, is a wetland area of 8445 hectares, including 2478 hectares of nature reserve and 564 hectares of marine park. Founded in 1986, it became an area of special ornithological protection in 1987 and an internationally important wetland zone in 1993. It is the second largest wetland sanctuary in the Mediterranean after the Camargue, and the second most important in Spain (after Doñana). Designated walking and cycling routes lead the visitor past extensive rice paddies, alongside canals, round fresh and salt-water lagoons and on to vast, sandy beaches.

The principal Parc Natural dels Ports information office is close to Tortosa, in the Avenida Val de Zafan, 43520 Roquetes, tel. 0034 977 50 08 45. This office has a very good permanent exhibition of all aspects of els Ports and usually has the key walking maps and other publications for sale.

There are two Parc Natural del Delta de l'Ebre Information centres: on the north side of the river at Ecomuseu, Carrer Doctor Marti Buera, 22 43580 Deltebre, tel. 0034 977 48 96 79; and on the south side of the river at Casa de Fusta (exhibition centre), Partida de la Cuixota 43870 Poble Nou del Delta, tel. 0034 977 26 10 22. The latter is adjacent to a very good restaurant.

For more information on the natural parks see www.gencat.cat, convert to English and then select els Ports or Delta de l'Ebre.

CLIMATE AND WHEN TO GO

The main areas covered in this guide are on the southern, south-eastern and eastern sides of the main els Ports massif and they benefit from a temperate Mediterranean climate which gives very good winter walking. Naturally, this becomes sub-Mediterranean at higher altitudes. Generally, the temperature at the summit of Mont Caro (1442m) is 5–10° lower than that in Tortosa. Also, some of the routes described here cross onto the northern and western flanks of the massif, which are influenced by the continental weather system and are therefore cooler and wetter.

Compared with winter walking in the UK a major consideration is the amount of daylight available. Due to the difference in time zones and the lower latitude, sunrise is at a similar local time but at mid-winter the daylight lasts some 1½hrs longer than in central England.

Overall, the major weather factor to take note of is wind. The prevailing wind during the winter is the

A dusting of December snow on Mont Caro, seen over olive trees

Tramontana from the north-west. This brings dry, clear weather but can be very strong. If you triple the forecast wind speed at Tortosa, you get a reasonable estimate of wind speed on the high ridges. During periods of high wind a characteristic cloud which hugs the summit ridge of the els Ports massif can be seen clearly from Tortosa. The local name for this cloud (translated) is 'the eyebrow'. In general, the Serras of Montsia and Cardó and also the coast are less affected by this wind, providing a choice of good alternative walks until it calms down. Easterly winds, which are fortunately much rarer, bring cloud and rain in from the sea. Sea fogs are also produced by easterly winds but these offer the opportunity on all three mountain groups of walking in clear sunshine above the clouds.

A very useful 10-day forecast for Tortosa can be found at www.weather.com, while the national Spanish meteorological service, at www.aemet.es, additionally provides seven-day forecasts for the main mountain villages. Click on 'Welcome' to access the English language version, then navigate to 'forecast', then 'location' and enter 'Tarragona' for the province, after which the individual villages can be selected. Some snowfall can be expected on high ground for, typically, four or five days during December and January but it rarely stays long. The AEMET site gives a snowline prediction but the actual amount of snow is usually less.

Altitude: 30m	Jan	Feb	Mar	Apr	May	Jun	Jul	Aug	Sep	Oct	Nov	Dec
Av. temp:	9.9	10.2	13.0	15.8	19.1	23.6	26.0	25.7	22.5	18.5	12.8	9.4
Day (max)	15.4	16.1	19.2	22.4	25.7	30.6	32.8	32.8	29.0	24.5	18.2	13.9
Night (min)	5.6	5.6	8.3	10.6	13.9	18.0	20.8	20.4	17.8	14.1	8.6	5.6
Hours of daylight[1]	9.6	10.6	11.9	13.3	14.5	15.1	14.8	13.8	12.5	11.1	9.9	9.2
Hours of sun	6.1	6.2	7.1	7.9	8.3	10.3	10.8	9.4	7.7	6.4	6.1	5.3
Days of rain/month	2	8	6	4	10	7	2	8	5	12	11	5
Rainfall (mm)	18.8	38.0	36.0	55.1	82.4	10.4	15.5	27.2	84.3	86.0	40.7	49.2
Wind speed (km/h)	10.7	8.8	11.6	9.6	9.0	8.6	9.3	9.5	8.5	7.4	9.8	11.4

[1]sunrise to sunset

The table above, compiled by the Observatori de l'Ebre from data recorded at its location in Roquetes (adjacent to Tortosa), gives averages for the past five years.

GEOLOGY AND GEOGRAPHY

The els Ports range and the satellite massifs of Montsia and Cardó rise steeply from sea level and comprise many variations on the theme of limestone. They are formed from a complex upthrust which straddles the Catalan Mediterranean and Iberian systems, with much faulting and significant overthrusts of the fault planes. In practical terms this has resulted in a dramatic, varied and complex landscape for walkers and climbers. The main ridges are predominantly dolomitic limestone, which forms spectacular cliffs and pinnacles on the eastern slopes facing the Mediterranean, and there are substantial outlying summits of more erosion-resistant rocks, such as lutites and coarser agglomerates, particularly on the western side. Weathering of these agglomerated rocks generally produces more rounded, sculptural forms reminiscent of gritstone. The extremely diverse nature of the terrain encountered throughout the region is because of the effect of local variations in the limestone and the availability of water. There are numerous springs that emerge where rainwater sinking through the limestone encounters a more impermeable layer. Some valleys have reliable streams but most water is sub-surface, only emerging in resurgences (*bufadors*) after heavy rain.

A broad plain rises gradually from the River Ebre towards the base of els Ports and adds substantial drama to the view of the mountains from Tortosa. This plain, planted with oranges and olives, is underlain by a coarse agglomerate rock. This is exposed around Tortosa, particularly on the approaches to the Suda Castle and around the adjacent historic fortifications. A similar agglomerate forms low cliffs on the coast, where wave erosion has shaped a series of small coves and picturesque headlands. Generally, the agglomerate is strongly bound together like a natural concrete and, from its appearance, is often called 'puddingstone'. In a number of places it has been eroded by wave action to reveal ancient coral.

In sharp contrast to the mountains, the Delta de l'Ebre is defined by its flatness, rarely rising more than two metres above sea level. In geological terms it is a very recent addition to the coastline, and was approximately a fifth of its present size in 2000BC. Its growth can be attributed to deforestation upstream, with the Romans being responsible for the first period of rapid expansion. The recent building of dams and control of the flow of the Ebre has practically halted growth of the Delta.

WILDLIFE

A wide range of habitats is found in the els Ports massif and this sustains a surprising variety of wild mammals, birds and reptiles.

Mammals

Among the most visible mammals are the Spanish ibex. These animals, recognisable by the huge curved

Forms characteristic of the western slopes with the sculptured shape of the Roques Benet behind (walk 3)

horns of the males, are both protected and controlled. Remarkably, the relatively small region of els Ports has in the region of 4000 ibex and they are encountered frequently on walks. An annual census is taken and their population has grown rapidly since the creation of the

Male ibex seen on the Solana route (Walk 5)

Reserva Nacional de Caça in 1966.

Wild boar are also very numerous and signs of their digging and rooting can be seen almost everywhere in the region. Since they are largely active at night they are frustratingly difficult to see. Their habits also make it impossible to carry out a census and the numbers are unknown, except that they are numerous, increasing and have to be controlled to prevent damage to the forest. Wild cats, otters, genets, foxes, badgers and martens are more timid and difficult to encounter but red squirrels can often be seen in the forested areas. These smaller mammals also thrive in the Cardó area.

Birds

The birdlife in the region is spectacular. Many raptors find good breeding and living conditions in the els Ports massif and Cardó areas, including griffon vultures, golden eagles, Bonelli's eagles, eagle owls, peregrine falcons and goshawks. Short-toed and booted eagles are summer nesting visitors. Choughs congregate around the high ridges and cols and ravens are frequently heard and seen. Swallows, swifts and martins swoop and glide at all levels, according to season.

Many smaller birds populate the forested areas, especially around the springs, which are often alive with birdsong. Many of these are familiar to British woodland walkers such as robins, chaffinches, nuthatches, tree creepers, thrushes, goldfinches and coal tits. Others are fairly rare in the UK: crossbills, blackcaps, firecrests, little and tawny owls, Sardinian and Dartford warblers and green and great-spotted woodpeckers. A few are spectacularly Mediterranean such as blue rock thrushes, hoopoes, orioles and bee-eaters (in summer only!).

In fact, dedicated birdwatchers find this a rich area to explore, particularly the Delta where numerous hides in strategic places overlook the fresh and saltwater lagoons (*bassas* in Catalan). The variety of resident and visiting birds on the Delta is famous but beyond the scope of this guide. More information on birds in both mountain and Delta areas can be found on the region's tourist board website www.terresdelebre.org. Select English language and then follow the links: 'Discover us', 'nature and eco-tourism' then 'ornithological tourism' or download the excellent birdwatching brochure. For guided birdwatching tours of varying lengths by local English-speaking experts see www.ebrotours.co.uk and www.andouinbirding.com. The former also gives up-to-date information on bird sightings.

Plants and flowers

Southern Catalunya is surprisingly green and visitors arriving by air often comment on the extent of the forests, especially over the uplands. Mediterranean and alpine species are well represented. Kermes or scrub oak and holly oak clothe the southern and eastern lower slopes together with box scrub. European fan palms, rosemary, lavender, thyme, broom,

(Clockwise from bottom left): Tree heather on la Moleta in November (Walk 9); Rosy garlic on the Montaspre ridge in April (Walk 2); Endemic fritillary, near the Balneari de Cardó in April (Walks 26 and 27)

gorse, tree heather and cistus cover the more open areas. Between 700m and 1000m the vegetation becomes sub-Mediterranean, with European black pine and Aleppo pine trees dominating, while tall Scots pines are found above 1000m. A special feature of els Ports is the nature reserve, protecting the most southerly beech trees in Europe and groves of yew trees – left over from a cooler and more humid epoch.

Spring flowers start as early as late February on the lower south-facing slopes and in protected areas. Violets, anemones and primulas are among the first woodland species to flower, while by early March open stony areas can be enlivened by bright patches of miniature daffodils. From this time on the cistus starts to bloom with huge pink flowers, an endemic butterwort can be found in damp places and the orchids start to emerge. These are just a few examples.

HISTORY, ARCHITECTURE AND CULTURE

People have lived in southern Catalunya since Palaeolithic times. Cave-dwelling hunter gatherers have left evidence in the form of bones in many places, including the Cova del Vidre (Walks 15 and 20). During the Neolithic period (around 3000BC to 50BC) Bronze Age and then Iron Age settlers began to create semi-permanent agricultural communities, using money and making pottery. The painted caves (*Covas Pintadas*) date from this time.

The first permanent settlements were created from 500BC to 200BC by the Iberians, so named by the Romans after the Iber (or Ebre) river. They settled mostly on the western and northern sides of the els Ports massif and notably at Horta de Sant Joan. It was the Romans who, recognising the strategic importance of the River Ebre, began the development of the city of Tortosa on the eastern side of the massif in the 3rd century. They built the acropolis of Dertosa on the site which later became the Suda castle and is now a Parador Hotel. It was under the Christian emperors of Rome that Tortosa first became a bishopric in the 4th century.

The Moorish occupation between the 8th and 12th centuries put an end to the power of the bishops but also brought about a transformation of both town and countryside. The Moors developed an irrigation system, starting with a weir (*assut*) at Xerta, turning the plain into rich agricultural land for olives, almonds and other crops. Castles were built on the plain and in the foothills of els Ports, around which small settlements grew to form villages. The Moors also began the exploitation of the forests of els Ports and developed Tortosa into a prosperous merchant city, making it their stronghold and capital of the area. The Suda castle was built and fortified; Tortosa then controlled the important river trade. Salt, timber, wheat

Looking over the extensive ramparts of the Suda Castle to els Ports

and local produce travelled downriver, while goods arriving from across the Mediterranean travelled upriver into the Iberian heartlands, and Tortosa extracted tolls in each direction. Under the Moorish *co-vivencia* Muslims, Jews and Christians lived peacefully, if not equally, together for 300–400 years, building a thriving economy in the region.

The Moorish period was brought to an end when Ramon Berenguer IV led the Christian reconquest of the area, capturing Tortosa in 1148 and placing it under the governance of the Knights Templar. The Templars also set up outposts in the castles and villages created by the Moors and over the next hundred years each village was granted its charter and a feudal system was established. The bishopric

was restored in Tortosa and grew in strength. Both Jews and Moors were required to convert to Christianity if they wished to remain. Those who chose not to either 'went underground' or were expelled in the 15th and 16th centuries. Tortosa's economic success continued throughout the Middle Ages and on into the 19th century despite being twice captured and occupied by the French (in 1708 and from 1811 to 1814).

During the Spanish Civil War Catalunya was the last province to fall to Franco's troops. The final battle in the hot summer of 1938, the Battle of the Ebro, was fought just upriver from Tortosa on the Serres de Pandols-Cavalls. It lasted 115 days and the loss of life on both sides and damage to villages and city were devastating. During Franco's ensuing dictatorship the Catalan language and culture was suppressed. Only after his death in 1975 and the establishment of democracy in 1978 were the Catalans able to speak their language publicly. From this point on they set about re-establishing their cultural life and restoring their historic architecture.

Today the area is called the Baix Ebre (lower Ebre) and Tortosa is its administrative and commercial capital. The Baix Ebre shares in the prosperity of present-day Catalunya and yet its heritage and traditions are still very much in evidence. Villages such as Paüls, Xerta and Mas de Barberans are still agricultural centres, producing olive oil, almonds and cherries as they did in Moorish times, but now they have tractors and also produce citrus fruits – lemons, satsumas and oranges. In Tortosa's ancient centre the buildings trace the city's history. There are remains of Roman pillars and a Moorish well and cemetery around the Parador. The old Jewish Quarter of Remolins is still at the foot of the Parador walls. The extensive walls and fortifications started by the Templars enclose the city's northern boundary. The 14th-century Bishop's Palace overlooking the river, the 16th-century Royal College (for the conversion of Moors to Christianity), the early 20th-century 'Modernista' style market hall and abattoir and, controversially, the Nationalist monument to the Battle of the Ebro in the middle of the river all attest to its vibrant history. For more

The ruins of the Mas de les Eres (Walk 25)

information on the history of Tortosa visit www.tortosaturisme.cat/en.

GETTING THERE

This is not an area covered by package holiday companies, despite the fact that it can be reached relatively easily from the UK by plane, train, coach, ferry or road.

By air

Reus airport is less than one hour's drive away. Only Ryanair operates during the winter walking season, with flights from a number of UK regional airports. Check www.ryanair.com for up-to-date information and booking. By car the simplest route from the airport to Tortosa is via the A7 toll motorway. Turn right out of the airport and then follow signs for Tarragona until diverted off to join the A7 towards Valencia. Leave the A7 at junction 40 and the C42 dual carriageway leads directly into Tortosa. A slower but very picturesque route follows the N420 to Mora la Nova, to join the C230 and travel south to Tortosa alongside the river. By public transport there just one direct bus per day, see www.hife.es for details.

Barcelona airport is approximately two hour's drive away and has many airlines serving London and other UK regional airports, including Easyjet, Jet2.com and British Airways. Aer Lingus has regular flights to Eire (Cork and Dublin). Leaving the airport by car look for signs for Sitges and

Castelldefels via the C32. This scenic motorway joins the main southbound A7 at St Vincenç de Calders and from here the route is as described previously.

Buses and trains travel between Barcelona and Tortosa but it is necessary to travel into the centre of Barcelona in order to access them. Check out www.hife.es for bus and www.renfe.es for train timetables. There is also a Rapid Bus from the airport to Tarragona for onward trains and buses to Tortosa. See www.barcelonatravelsite.com.

By rail

Rail travel is comfortable using Eurostar to Paris and then taking the Elipsos Trenhotel overnight to Barcelona Estacio de França. See www.spanish-rail.co.uk, www.renfe.es and www.raileurope.co.uk for information and bookings. From here there is a direct but slow (2½hrs) connecting train to Tortosa.

By coach

At 27hrs it is a long coach journey from London to Barcelona but it can be done. See www.eurolines.com for information and booking.

By ferry

Travelling by sea is an alternative, especially for anyone wanting to bring their own car. Brittany Ferries operate crossings from Portsmouth and Plymouth to Santander, while P&O cross between Portsmouth and Bilbao.

GETTING AROUND

Some form of personal transport is strongly recommended as it is not possible to get around much of the walking area by public transport. There are buses between the villages and Tortosa but often they are only once or twice a day. Also many walks start from access roads reaching well into the mountains. Rental cars can be booked in advance from the usual companies (such as Hertz, Avis and Budget) at both Barcelona and Reus airports. It is also possible to hire a car in Tortosa. See www.turismetortosa.com for a list of car hire companies, although none can be booked online. The same website also provides a link to a cycle hire company.

The best solution for those who really do not want to drive is to arrange transport with an organisation that offers guided walks, such as Ebro Tours. See www.ebrotours.co.uk for contact details.

WHERE TO STAY

Tortosa is the main business and administrative centre of the area and makes a good central base for all three walking areas. Its historic centre, full of medieval and renaissance buildings, is fascinating to wander around and its market hall, adjacent to the broad river, is full of local produce and has lively tapas bars. There are pavement cafés, bars and many good restaurants in Tortosa but it is a busy place. Apart from the Parador Hotel in the Suda Castle, its hotels reflect its business character rather than its history. For rural peace and quiet there are a few small hotels, plus bed and breakfast and rental properties that give good access to the starts of the walks and are not too far from the restaurants.

Hotels

All the hotels below give good access to the walking areas. Some can be booked online in English at www.booking.com and it is worth checking other hotel booking agencies for offers.

Suda Castle Parador Hotel ****, Tortosa 0034 977 44 44 50 www.parador.es

Hotel Corona Plaça ***, Plaça Corona d'Arago, Tortosa 0034 977 58 04 33 www.bshotels.es

Hotel Berenguer IV ***, Christofol Despuig 36, Tortosa 0034 977 44 08 16 www.hotelberenguer.com

Hotel Tortosa Parc **, Conde de Banuelos 10, Tortosa 0034 977 44 61 12 www.hoteltortosaparc.com

Hotel Rural Panxampla, Carretera d'Alfara, els Reguers 0034 977 47 41 35 www.elcellerdenpanxampla.com

Hotel Pepo, Carrer Piscines 1, Benifallet 0034 977 46 22 00 www.hotelpepo.com

For luxury, style and a Michelin star, at a corresponding price:

Hotel Spa Villa Retiro *****, Carrer dels Molins 2, Xerta 0034 977 47 30 03 www.hotelvillaretiro.com

For overnight accommodation on the two-day Walk 25 crossing from Sant Roc to Arnes try **Vilar Rural dels Ports**, Arnes 0034 977 43 57 37 www.vilarsrurals.com; or **Can Barrina Sta Madrona 27**, Arnes 0034 977 43 51 37 www.canbarrina.net.

Rental properties and B&Bs

There are a number of English-run rental properties and B&Bs which can be booked from the UK but it is important to check whether they are well-placed for the walking areas. Tortosa, Roquetes, Raval de Jesus, els Reguers, Benifallet, Aldover and Alfara de Carles are all useful locations. Also, the normal emphasis is on summer lets. Heating and hot water are important for winter walking. Ebro Tours (www.ebrotours.co.uk or tel. 0034 977 26 73 82) have two houses which fulfil both criteria. It is also worth checking Brighter Spain (www.brighterspain.com or tel. 0034 619 77 24 92), www.ownersdirect.co.uk (click on Tarragona and then Tortosa) and www.ebroriverrentals.com, remembering to query the heating arrangements.

For links to village accommodation see www.terresdelebre.com, in English. Select 'lodging' to find village by village listings. On the els Ports side of the river (west bank) the villages with good access to the walking areas are Paüls and Xerta to the north, Mas de Barberans to the south and Alfara de Carles in the centre. On the east bank of the river, Benifallet,

The village of Paüls, in its rocky amphitheatre

although quite northerly, is adjacent to a useful river crossing.

Refuges

There are some refuges in els Ports Parc Natural and one in the Cardó but none in the Montsia walking area. In els Ports, the Refugi de Caro (Walks 12–14, and passed en route to Walks 15 and 16) has a guardian in the summer and on occasional weekends (tel. 0034 977 26 71 28). It offers shelter and a fireplace all year but no water. The Refugi de Font Nova (Walks 9–11) requires a key obtained in advance (tel. 0034 977 47 36 64). The Refugi de les Clotes (Walks 5 and 7) is unguarded and gives good shelter but no water.

There are two additional refuges in els Ports which are not passed on the walks in this guide but which are marked on maps: the Refugi de Fontferrera (guarded in summer and weekends; shelter and water at other times: tel. 0034 977 26 71 10) and the Refugi del Mas del Frare (key needed: tel. 0034 630 518 254).

The Refugi de la Font del Teix in the Cardó (Walk 26) is unguarded but well appointed and has water nearby. It is open all year.

Other mountain accommodation

The Restaurant del Port at l'Esquirol near to Mont Caro (tel. 0034 977 26 71 43) has rooms but its opening times are unpredictable. The residencia Casa de Pages 'Ca les Barberes' at Paüls (tel. 0034 977 43 56 29) offers year-round hostel type accommodation.

There are no particular health and safety issues beyond those common to European mountainous areas. The emergency phone number for police, fire, ambulance and mountain rescue is 112 and English can be used. There is good mobile phone network coverage throughout and carrying a phone is recommended as there are few other walkers, no refuge guardians and infrequent patrols by els Ports rangers.

There is an emergency department at Tortosa Hospital, the Verge de la Cinta on the Carrer Esplanetes, tel. 0034 977 51 91 00, clearly visible above the town. There is a health centre (Centre de Salut) next door to the Tortosa tourist office on the Avinguda Generalitat, tel. 0034 977 51 0018.

There are three types of police: the Guardia Civil, the Policia Local and the Mossos. Broadly speaking the Guardia handle national security, serious fraud and protection of the Spanish state, the Mossos are concerned with the protection of individuals and property in their area and public order and the Policia Local look after traffic, crime prevention and local crimes. All would help in an emergency. Victims of theft or harassment or other criminal damage in or around Tortosa should contact either:

- The **Mossos**; Carrer Comers, 87, tel. 0034 977 503 685; or
- The **Policia Local**; Passeig Joan Moreira, 3, tel. 0034 977 449 731

LANGUAGE

The local people of this area are proudly Catalan but will happily speak Spanish to foreigners. English is spoken in the larger hotels and tourist offices but not as widely as in the more developed Spanish resorts. Mime, sketching and 'spanglish' words accompanied by a smile are all accepted means of communication, especially if preceded by one of the basic Catalan greetings:

¡Hola! (pronounced 'ola'), Bon Dia (for the morning) or Bona Tarde (for the late afternoon/evening and pronounced 'bona tarda'). Conversations can be concluded with goodbye – Adeu (pronounced 'ad<u>e</u>yoo').

Appendix C gives a translation of Catalan mountain terms.

MONEY

The currency is the Euro and credit cards are widely accepted but a passport may also be needed for confirmation of identity, especially in supermarkets. Multilingual ATM machines are easy to find in Tortosa, always associated with banks.

FOOD AND DRINK

A wealth of local produce, combined with historical cultural diversity, has produced an exceptional cuisine in this part of Catalunya. Rick Stein was moved to say ¡Me gusta mucho! Citrus fruits, cherries, almonds and olives from the river plain, rice, seafood, eels, duck, rabbit and vegetables from the Delta, cured ham, sausages and game from the mountains

Crossing the slopes of the Solana (Walk 5)

and, of course, a bewildering array of fish are all on offer. A walk through Tortosa market gives an idea of the variety and quality available. One can be confident of having a very good meal in virtually any restaurant, even the simplest village restaurant – if one is not wholly vegetarian. If this is so, the only option, sadly, is self-catering.

The best value is the *Menu del Dia*, sometimes only served at lunchtime. This three-course meal, usually including wine and coffee, will cost between €12 and €20 in Tortosa. Generally the village restaurants are cheaper. The larger restaurants will usually offer a written menu, sometimes in English, (for a la carte meals ask to see *la carta*), but the simpler restaurants may present their menu verbally in Catalan, or in Spanish if requested.

Local specialities include:

- *Escudella* – a hearty soup of vegetables with pieces of veal or pork and sausage
- *Pa amb tomaquet* – bread or toast spread with olive oil, garlic and tomato
- *Escalivada* – roasted peppers, aubergines and courgettes
- *Esqueixada* – thin slices of salt or smoked cod in parsley and olive oil
- *Paella Marinera* – rich rice dish with fish and seafood
- *Paella Mixta* – rich rice dish with seafood and pieces of rabbit and pork
- *Arros negre* – black rice – rice cooked with cuttle fish ink
- *Fideua* – noodles cooked in rich fish stock with seafood
- *Suquet* – fish cooked in stock with potatoes
- *Ternasco* – lamb shank
- *Butifarra* – Catalan pork sausage often served with beans
- *Morcilla* – black pudding
- *Baldana* – sausage made with rice, meat, pine nuts, garlic and spices.

A full treatment of local cuisine demands a guidebook of its own. The best advice is: be bold and try it!

Food and drink for walking can be bought at any of the four supermarkets or smaller shops in Tortosa. The supermarkets are open all day and well into the evening, whereas the smaller shops close between 1330 and 1700. However, all are closed on Sundays. There are also small shops, restaurants and bars in some of the villages closer to the starts of the walks but their opening hours can be unreliable. It is worth noting that restaurants are generally open for lunch between 1330 and 1600 and in the evening from 2030 until late.

Paüls (Walks 1–4) has a baker, a butcher and a small grocery shop as well as three café-bars. Els Reguers (Walks 4–8) has several grocery shops, bakers, bars and restaurants. Alfara de Carles (also Walks 4–8) has two grocery shops and two bakers,

29

plus four restaurants in the village, one bull farm restaurant on the road to el Toscar and another in el Toscar itself (summer and feast days only). Xerta (Walks 9–11) has grocery shops, bakers, bars and restaurants.

L'Esquirol, adjacent to Mont Caro (Walks 12–16) has two restaurants but no shops. Mas de Barberans (Walks 20–24) has three grocery shops, two bakers, two butchers, two restaurants and a couple of bars.

For walks in the Cardó, food can be obtained en route in Rasquera, which has a number of food shops, bars and restaurants. The Montsia walks are close to the fishing port of Sant Carles de la Rapita which has a wide range of shops, bars and restaurants.

There are springs (*fonts*) in all three walking areas and they are marked on the maps. However, water should be carried as some springs disappear in dry weather and others can be muddied by animals. In general if the water is clear it is drinkable.

WHAT TO TAKE

T-shirts and light trousers are the normal walking gear for this area but, as in any other serious mountains, conditions can change rapidly, especially wind speed and wind chill factor. In the winter months it is prudent to carry light waterproofs/wind-proofs, fleece, gloves and a warm hat but expect to use them rarely. Otherwise, layering is, as usual, the key. A hat with a brim

to shade the eyes plus sunglasses are, happily, essential equipment throughout the winter. Trousers are generally preferable to shorts, to give some protection from the occasional spiky vegetation. Lightweight walking boots are sufficient, if they have a good cleated sole. Those accustomed to walking with trekking poles will find them useful. A 35-litre daysack should be ample to carry all the spare clothing, food and at least a litre of water. For those susceptible to sunburn it is best to carry sun-block as a matter of course.

WAYMARKING AND ACCESS

All the walks in the guide follow established routes; in fact, the complex and vertiginous nature of most of the routes makes improvisation very difficult, if not dangerous. Many of the paths are very old, having been established by shepherds to move their flocks between watering places and the many small patches of high mountain pasture. When walking them you will be impressed by the long and patient exploration that must have been needed to find the best and, sometimes, only possible route.

On most routes essential guidance is provided by waymarks. These take the forms of paint marks, cairns and, at important junctions, small metal plate signs bolted to rocks in (mostly) prominent places. On the simpler walks the Parc Natural dels Ports organisation has erected signposts. In addition, there are the conventional European footpath markers:

- red and white for the long-distance GR paths of more than 50km
- yellow and white for regional PR paths of 10 to 50km
- green and white (rarely) for local paths of less than 10km
- blue stars for the *Estels* multi-day circuit of els Ports.

Both law and local attitudes give the walker a very free 'right to roam'. Tracks barred with chains are largely intended to exclude vehicles. Areas

intended to be kept private are usually well enclosed by fences and clearly labelled. None of the walks in this guide takes the walker onto property where privacy is an issue.

Otherwise, the norms of walking apply: close gates, take rubbish home and, particularly in this dry terrain, never start a fire. A particular point to note is that camping is not permitted in the Parc Natural. There are a number of refuges dotted about but check with the Parc Natural office in Roquetes for up-to-date information on access since some require keys.

A very unusual aspect of walking in els Ports is the pasturing of bulls. This is a traditional activity which has been accommodated within the

The Font del Montsagre de l'Horta (Walk 1)

Parc Natural framework. In the pasturing areas signs are encountered which warn of 'Wild Bulls' or *Bous Braus*. When encountered the bulls should not be approached, although they also seem keen to maintain their distance. By all reports, walkers and bulls co-exist peacefully on this basis.

HUNTING AND HOW TO AVOID IT

Hunting is permitted in the Reserva Nacional de Caça, the broader Parc area and the surrounding countryside. It plays an important role in maintaining sustainable, healthy populations of ibex and wild boar. Within the reserve, the park rangers organise boar hunts or *batuda* and they cordon off the area they are using and place signs at entry points to warn walkers. It is strongly advised to take heed of these warnings and choose another walk. A boar hunt covers a lot of ground and involves a large team of people with guns and dogs chasing large, fast and dangerous (no brakes, sharp tusks) animals downhill. They are not discreet affairs, so the chances of walking into one without being aware of it are very low. The hunting of ibex within the reserve, on the other hand, is a quieter, altogether safer affair of two or three hunters, guided by a ranger who has already selected the weaker or older animals to be culled.

On the edges of the Parc, where land is privately owned, wild boar hunting is also permitted under

Mature pine woods on the way to the Coll d'Atans (Walk 1)

restrictions imposed by a legal framework. These areas are always signed by *Area Privada de Caça* and local associations manage and control the hunting here. Again, it is a legal requirement for them to place warning notices. Also on privately owned land there is considerable ad hoc rough shooting – individuals wandering, noisily, with a shotgun.

The season for wild boar hunting is October to February inclusive but it is restricted to weekends within the Reserva Nacional de Caça (essentially the Parc Natural) and to weekends, Thursdays and 'feast days' (bank holidays) in the Area Privada de Caça. Permanent metal signs identifying one or the other are posted throughout the walking area. Ibex are hunted during April and May and again during October, November and December, Mondays to Fridays within the Reserva but all week outside. It is important to note that in five years of walking in the area we have had to change our walk plan only once to avoid a *batuda* and have only once encountered ibex hunters. It is clear that only a proportion of the opportunities for hunting are actually taken.

MAPS

This guide is intended to be used in conjunction with walking maps produced by Editorial Piolet. These provide, within the limitations of the 1:25,000 and 1:30,000 scales, a good depiction of the walking terrain. Discrepancies between the maps and routes 'on the ground' are dealt with both on the sketch maps and in the text. The following are useful maps:

• Estels del Sud, La Travessa del Massis dels Ports
• El Port Mapes Excursionistes (two sheets, sold as a pair)
• Cardó and Rasquera.

The Estels del Sud map is designed to accompany a multi-day circuit of els Ports and gives guidance in four languages including English. All the maps are available as both hardcopy and CDs and can be purchased online from the publisher at www.editorialpiolet.com (Catalan only) and from the main Tortosa bookshop at www.la2deviladrich.cat/public/en, which has an English language option.

The Institut Cartografic de Catalunya produces maps of the area at 1:50,000, which can be bought in the UK. The scale is inappropriate for walking the Baix Ebre (9) and Montsia (22) sheets are useful as detailed road maps. There is also online access to 1:10,000 maps at www.icc.es, but these lack essential footpath information.

USING THE GUIDE

A route summary table is given in Appendix A with an indication of difficulty, the ease of route-finding, exposure and any requirement for scrambling.

Directions relating to rivers and *barrancs* use the 'true left bank' or 'true right bank' convention: that is, the left or right bank when facing downstream.

Walking times

The walking times given at the beginning of each walk are just that – the time spent moving. Naturally, the times given are those taken based on our own experience. After a few walks using the guide you will know whether you are faster or slower, and can make due allowance. The overall time for a walk will, of course, depend on time out for breaks, photographs and simply looking at flora, fauna and the changing views. Even after five years of familiarity with these mountains we typically take 6hrs over a route with 4hrs of walking time, particularly on warm, sunny days.

Route-finding

The nature of the terrain dictates that most walking is done on paths but this does not mean that the way forward is always obvious. Paths go off in unexpected directions and lack of use can make the trace on the ground indistinct – hence the three grades. If a walk is graded ● the path is always clear on the ground and other guidance, such as cairns and signposts, will confirm the route. Walks graded ●● will have sections where finding

the way forward demands some ability to read the terrain with the aid of the route description, sketch map and recommended area map. Grade ●●● is reserved for walks where the complexity of the terrain and the obscurity of some of the paths make navigation difficult, where there are substantial pathless sections and where the vertiginous nature of the terrain makes accurate navigation essential for safety. For each walk with the ●●● grade the specific nature of the navigational problems will be described at the beginning of the walk.

Scrambling

Any scrambling associated with the walks is easy or avoidable. Rock-climbing skills in the line of a route are neither assumed nor needed. The

The lower ladder of the Escarrisó de Borosa (Walk 20)

Overlapping crags and ridges disappear into the distance

only exception is Walk 18, which includes more serious scrambling. The grading is concerned with the amount of scrambling on a route, since routes with frequent scrambles are more physically demanding than those with none.

Exposure

The vertiginous nature of much of the terrain in these mountains demands that this issue is taken seriously. The route of a walk graded ● will not go near the edges of cliffs or over very steep ground. However, this does not exclude a substantial ascent or the reward of fine views. The ●● grade is for walks where the paths cross steep ground or skirt around the edges of substantial drops. The emphasis here is on feeling very much on the edge

of things but from a secure position. A walk graded ●●● will have sections where looking down from a height is combined with being on steep ground. A fall is likely to have serious consequences and this grade requires confidence in moving over narrow paths, rough ground and scrambling in high places.

Finding the walks

This can be an adventure in itself for some of the walks! The access routes are unclear on the available maps and poorly signposted, if at all. The approximate locations of the starts are shown on the Location of Walks map, for use in conjunction with the detailed directions given in Appendix B. All the walk starts can be reached by a conventional road vehicle,

35

Paths find their way through apparently impossible cliff-scapes (Walk 13)

although two are on tracks where a less than average ground clearance could be a problem: the approach to la Caramella (Walks 17–19); and the Caro–Fredes track (Walk 16). Both have some particularly rough sections.

Warning

Mountain walking can be a dangerous activity carrying a risk of personal injury or death. It should be undertaken only by those with a full understanding of the risks and with the training and experience to evaluate them. While every care and effort has been taken in the preparation of this guide, the user should be aware that conditions can be highly variable and can change quickly, materially affecting the seriousness of a mountain walk. Therefore, except for any liability which cannot be excluded by law, neither Cicerone nor the author accept liability for damage of any nature (including damage to property, personal injury or death) arising directly or indirectly from the information in this book.

To call out the Mountain Rescue, ring the international emergency number 112: this will connect you via any available network. Once connected to the emergency operator, ask for the police.

WALK 1

Punta de l'Aigua

Difficulty	Route-finding ●● Scrambling ●● Exposure ●●
Total ascent	900m
Time	4hrs 30mins (plus 25mins for the summit detour to Punta de l'Aigua)
Distance	13km
Start	Paüls
Maps	El Port Nord, Editorial Piolet, 1:30,000

For full directions to start, see Appendix B.

This circular route starts in the picturesque hill village of Paüls. Clear, mostly waymarked, paths lead the walker through the rich and varied terrain of the northern els Ports, from olive and cherry terraces, up through a complex area of overhanging cliffs and steep valleys and onto the open grassy pasture of the Montsagre or sacred mountain. There are four cols to pass over, providing increasingly dramatic walking and views. From the third and highest col, a detour can be made to the summit of the Punta de l'Aigua with its 360° views. After a fourth col, a very good descent path leads back to Paüls.

Leave the Plaça Major on the steep street by the right side of the town hall which, after a few minutes, reaches the cemetery. Take the road to the right of the **cemetery**, following blue markers. At the back of the cemetery the road forks again. This junction has a handsome metal signpost, a local feature which appears in the most unexpected places. Following signs for Montsagre d'Horta and Coll Gilaberta, take the right fork and stay with the main track, leaving the village by the side of olive and cherry plantations. ▸ After 10mins the routes divide at a junction with a second metal signpost. Take the right track to follow **GR171** and, after approximately 50m,

The waymarking on this track is both blue for the Estels tour of els Ports and red and white for the GR171 long-distance path.

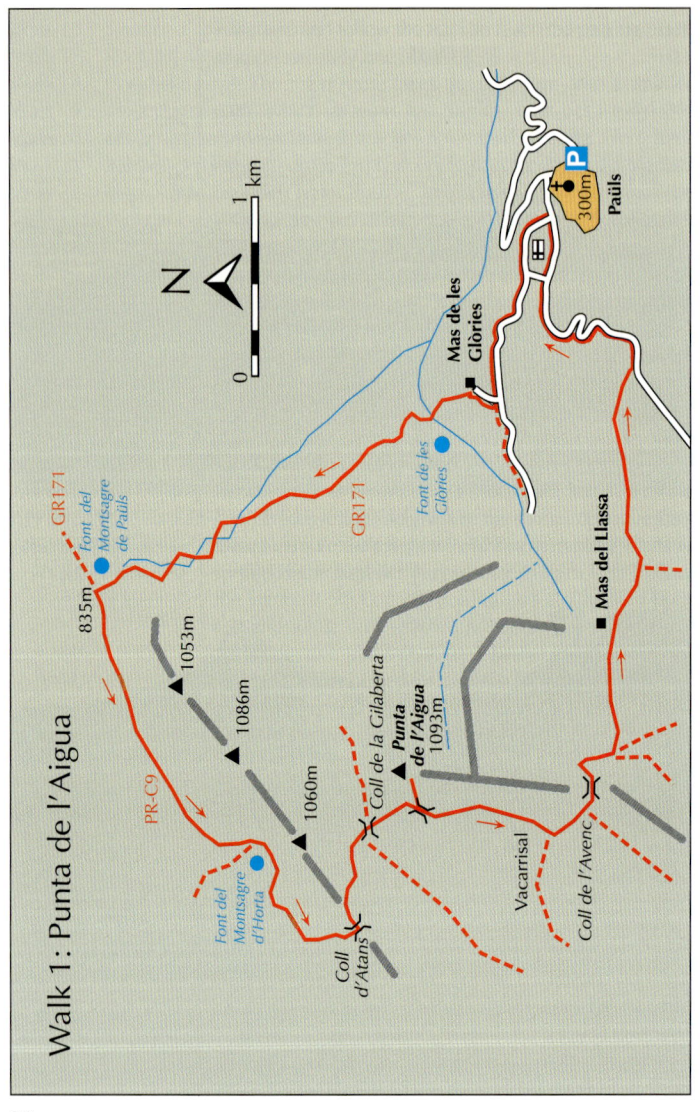

Walk 1: Punta de l'Aigua

turn left onto a path with a clear red and white marker visible.

Very soon another track is joined. Turn right and descend for 50m, leading to a junction marked with a cairn and a red and white marker. Here turn left onto a path which descends into the valley on zigzags, by the side of terraces planted with olives. Cross a small stream at the bottom of the valley on stepping stones, some 17mins from the start of the walk.

The route now ascends to join a track; follow it to the right for a few minutes to reach a wire fence. Leave the track by turning left onto a red and white waymarked path and climb beyond the village fields to enter an increasingly wild region of steep valleys and cliffs some 10mins later. Navigation here is not difficult but there are sharp changes of direction amongst boulders to look out for. About 35mins from the start the path enters a cirque with dramatically overhanging cliffs and passes a shallow cave where, after wet weather, a waterfall tumbles through a hole in the roof.

The path exits the cirque through large boulders and then climbs, steeply in places, zigzagging through pine and oak woodland. About an hour from the start the path enters a valley and descends slightly, to converge with and cross a stream bed. A few minutes further on upstream it crosses back, where the continuation is only marked by a cairn. The red and white markers re-commence after a few minutes. There are two further crossings, both clear, the second of which is reached around 25mins after entering the valley. The path now rises on the left side of the valley to emerge onto an unexpectedly lush and grassy area and continues alongside a stream for a few minutes, reaching the **Font del Montsagre de Paüls**, about 1½hrs from the start. ▶

Turning left onto PR-C9, yellow and white markers lead along a high grassy valley. The path rises gently through the pastoral landscape and then crosses some inclined limestone pavement to reach a wood. Just before entering the denser woodland there is a Reserva Nacional de Caça sign on a tree and, facing it, a cairn

Here a signpost marks the junction of footpaths GR171 and PR-C9.

Leaving the Font del Montsagre de Paüls

and yellow and white marker. Turn left here and then right after 20m to enter the wood on a clear path. Old eroded yellow and white markers appear after some 200m to confirm the direction. Leaving the trees, the path rises gently onto a high escarpment overlooking the Aragon plain, with the town of Horta de Sant Joan and the rounded rocky tops of the Muntanya Santa Barbara in the middle distance.

The path then drops to the **Font del Montsagre d'Horta** in a small valley headed by cliffs. Here another signpost points the way on to the Coll de la Gilaberta. After 10mins or so the path veers left, away from the line of the Montsagre d'Horta escarpment, following the yellow and white markers up and over a small rock band to reach the **Coll d'Atans**.

Lines of ridges disappear into the distance on the right and on the left the land falls away down to Paüls.

The 360° panorama from the Coll d'Atans reveals the drama of els Ports: below, the wooded Coll de la Gilaberta, ahead the steep rock of the Punta de l'Aigua. ◄ The path now descends left over rocks to the **Coll de la Gilaberta**, reached some 50mins from the Font del Montsagre de Paüls. Here a metal signpost points directly onwards to

Vacarissal. Two paths start in this direction and either can be used as they join later, although the left-hand path is favoured with cairns and yellow and white waymarks. About 10mins from the junction the now single path rises diagonally across steep rocky terrain towards a clear notch in the skyline, effectively an unofficial col. At the col there is a yellow and white marker and old directions in red paint, including one for the summit of the Punta de l'Aigua.

To visit the summit the route starts with a scramble up the ridge for about 50m, when it is possible to move to the right and gain a path leading up steeply into woodland. This rises, after 10mins, to a dip in the summit ridge. A path to the left leads to the highest point of the **Punta de l'Aigua** while to the right there is a remarkable airy ridge from which it is possible to look down 750m onto the village of Paüls.

After returning from the summit by the same route, the path, still waymarked in yellow and white, continues straight on, descending steeply over rocks and stony ground. After about 12mins from the col the path rises to cross a subsidiary ridge of the Punta and then descends more gently. After 30mins the path leads to **Vacarissal**. In this small, grassy valley there is a junction of paths and another signpost.

Starting in the direction signposted Paüls, the path rises through a small valley to reach a junction where the route turns left, abandoning the PR-C9 and its yellow and white markers. The new path continues to rise, guided by cairns, up to the **Coll d'Avenc**. Turn left along the top of the escarpment here, until the path starts to descend after about 50m. This excellent path descends gently to the left through pine woods and then by a series of zigzags down to a T-junction some 15mins after leaving Vacarissal. Turn left and continue for 30mins when the path converges with a track and in a little while passes a restored *mas* (farm). The track ends at a junction with a concrete and asphalt road after a futher 8mins; turn left along this road to reach the cemetery above Paüls after about 20mins to complete the circuit.

PAÜLS – A TYPICAL HILL VILLAGE

Paüls is a compact hill village some 16km north-west of Tortosa, surrounded by an amphitheatre of ridges and peaks. Its story is typical of the outlying communities of the Baix Ebre. The origins of Paüls go back at least to Roman times but its castle was built under the Moorish occupation of Al-Andalus in the 9th century. The church of Santa Maria is, in fact, built on the foundations of the original mosque. Paüls was an important strategic location for both the Moors and the Christians who conquered it in 1149. It was rich in natural resources, especially water, timber and agricultural land, and it remains so to this day. Sheep, cows and goats are grazed on its rich pastures and its fertile, well-watered land supports the cultivation of olives, cherries, almonds, vines, cereals, carobs and vegetables.

The village gained its charter in 1293 when the local baron, Joan Despuig, granted its inhabitants the right to live, farm, pasture, hunt and cut timber in perpetuity, in exchange for '300 sous of good money' to be paid every year at Christmas time. Paüls alternately flourished and suffered over the following six centuries, as peaceful times alternated with the frequent conflicts that swept through Spain. During the Carlist Wars in the first half of the 19th century the population was decimated and the castle destroyed. Later, the Civil War caused a mass migration during the period of the final, dreadful Battle of the Ebre. But, between these events, the population recovered and created an almost entirely self-sufficient community of 1241 inhabitants, with its own flour mill and brick factory and 14 olive oil mills.

In 2010 Paüls has a relatively stable population of 632 inhabitants and its economy is based on agriculture and tourism. It is famous for the quality of its cherries and holds an annual cherry festival during the last weekend in May.

(inset) The church of Santa Maria, Paüls

WALK 2
Montaspre ridge

Difficulty	Route-finding ●● Scrambling ● Exposure ●●
Total ascent	750m
Time	3hrs 40mins (plus 30mins for the summit detour to la Coscollosa)
Distance	13km
Start	Paüls
Map	El Port Nord, Editorial Piolet, 1:30,000

For full directions to start, see Appendix B.

The ridge that separates the hill villages of Paüls and Alfara de Carles is even less frequented by walkers than the main els Ports massif, yet it has a charm and drama of its own. The approach from Paüls, on small lanes and tracks through olive, cherry and almond plantations, has an aura of traditional cultivation stretching back to medieval times. After a climb through woodland, the route emerges under the steep cliffs guarding the Montaspre ridge before finding its way up a stony gully to reach the summit of la Coscollosa. The circuit then follows the main ridge, visiting both sides to give tremendous views of els Ports, the river plain and the distant sea.

The walk begins at the lower end of Paüls and takes the road to Sant Roc. After 4mins or so turn left onto a smaller surfaced road which leads down, past a restored stone barn, to reach a T-junction 8mins later. Turning left here the road crosses a dry *barranc* and, after passing several unsurfaced tracks to the right and left reaches, in about 5mins, a track on the right which has a concrete surface.

Turn right onto this track. The concrete surface soon ends and the track continues, climbing past a *casita* on the right to enter woodland of scrub oak and pine. Zigzags

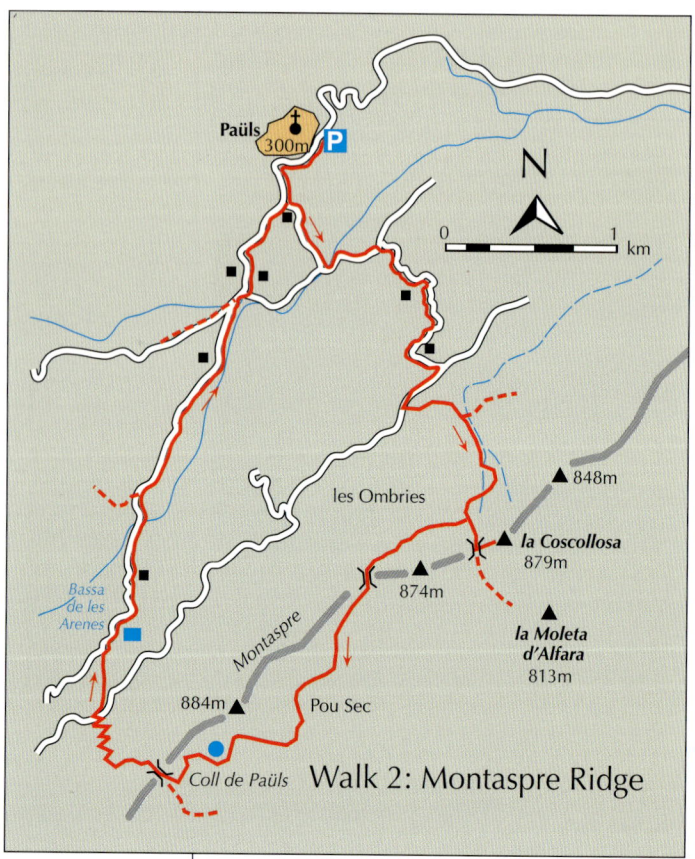

Walk 2: Montaspre Ridge

up through terraces lead to an apparent end of the track at a flat area below a fenced plantation, about 30mins from the start of the walk. Ignore the apparent ploughed earth track to the left and turn right to cross the flat area and find a small footpath leading from it. Overgrown to start with, this soon widens into a track and continues climbing to cross a field planted with olive, almond and cherry trees. Less than a minute later, the track passes

The Montaspre ridge from Paüls, with olive trees in the foreground

an old farmhouse with a water cistern and stone picnic tables. Pass round to the front of the farmhouse and follow the grassy access track which leads on up into the trees and then soon joins a broad forestry track (45mins from the start) onto which you turn right. ▶

Here it is possible to see red squirrels and occasionally ibex, as well as a variety of woodland birds.

After about 8mins there is a crossroads junction; take a small path to the left marked with a cairn to climb uphill and then contour round the hillside. Veering right the path now passes through a rocky gap and ascends a shallow barranc to reach a junction some 10mins from leaving the forestry track. Ignore the well-cairned and obvious path climbing up to the left in favour of a smaller path (also cairned) which continues up the barranc to climb up through **les Ombries** of Montaspre – the shady, north-facing slopes of the ridge.

After 12mins the cairned path leads up to the left, to leave the barranc and cross into another, before climbing on grass to a rock-filled valley where two cairns indicate an oblique right turn. Now the path enters trees and climbs a shoulder to re-enter the first barranc at a rocky amphitheatre. After passing the ruins of a stone

45

animal pen the cairned path climbs up steeply to the left, towards an old drystone wall with a cairn on top. Climbing through the wall another cairn can be seen directly ahead, with the path leading up a scree-filled gully towards an obvious col on the ridge above. The route makes its way up the right edge of the lower part of this scree to find a T-junction with a yellow and white waymarked path, marked with a cairn. ◀ There is now a choice of continuing up the gully to the summit of la Coscollosa (30mins there and back) or taking the right turn to continue the circuit.

This point is reached some 45mins after leaving the forestry track.

To visit the summit a clear path finds an easy way up the scree of the gully and then veers left to emerge on grass and reach a col after 10mins. From here a number of paths lead up to the left, to reach the summit of **la Coscollosa** in 5mins. Retrace the route to descend and return to the T-junction to continue the circuit.

Emerging from the scree gully onto the summit ridge of la Coscollosa

The walk now follows the yellow and white way-marked footpath. Descending slightly to begin with, the path stays high above steep ground, crossing a band of steep scree some 10mins from the T-junction. It

then reaches another col beyond the steep cliffs of the Montaspre after 5mins where it crosses the ridge. ▶ Cairns and yellow and white waymarks confirm the direction of the clear path as it continues on the left-hand (south) side of the ridge. After a few minutes the way-marks end but the path is visible on the ground and has occasional cairns as it contours round the hillside. Some 20mins from the col the path traverses down into the shallow barranc of **Pou Sec** (dry well) headed by cliffs, and then climbs steeply to cross a shoulder ahead. ▶

Some 40mins from the Pou Sec barranc the path drops down over a small rockband and descends some scree to reach a water trough in a grassy bowl about 5mins later. A stone structure at one end of the trough contains a water cistern with a small door. Drinking water can be taken from here. Leaving the *font*, the cairned path climbs up towards the ridge then contours round and descends slightly, to join the red and white waymarked GR171 at the **Coll de Paüls**, some 15mins later. From here the path finds a clever way down the steep and dramatic descent to the valley. After 12mins it passes through an old fence and enters a broad scree-filled gully, making its way down the screes to reach a signposted crossroads with a track some 10mins later.

The GR171 route carries straight on in the direction of Paüls, passing a swimming pool-sized water reservoir, the **Bassa de les Arenes**. Immediately after passing it the path joins a track and continues on in the same direction, dropping down into the valley and crossing a shallow ford. After this turn right to continue on small lanes, following the red and white waymarks all the way back to Paüls.

There are extensive views over the Ebre valley to the sea beyond from the ridge.

Looking back gives good views of the Montaspre ridge, la Coscollosa beyond it and the fortress-like summit of la Moleta to its right.

WALK 3

Moleta de les Canals circuit and summit ridge

Difficulty	*Circuit*: Route-finding ●●
	Scrambling ● Exposure ●
	Ridge: Route-finding ●●●
	Scrambling ●● Exposure ●●
Total ascent	750m for the circuit, 650m for the ridge
Time	4hrs for the circuit, 3hrs 20mins for the ridge
Distance	11km for the circuit, 8km for the ridge
Start	Ermita de Sant Roc
Maps	Either Estels del Sud, Editorial Piolet, 1:25,000 (preferred) or El Port Nord, Editorial Piolet, 1:30,000

For full directions to start, see Appendix B.

Both options for this walk – the circuit and the ridge alternative – take in contrasting scenery and terrain, plus some dramatic views. Those from the Moleta de les Canals are exceptional. For the most part the circuit is on clear well-made tracks and paths, with just one section where some navigational care is needed. In contrast, the variant has no obvious traces on the ground and attention to the terrain is the key to success. Where the two options diverge from each other the circuit passes over to the north-west slopes of the els Ports massif and becomes, for a while, a valley walk.

Circuit route

Leave the picnic site of Sant Roc by the track that continues directly from the entrance road. After about 50m a right turn onto an unmarked track leads past some buildings. The chain across the track and the 'private property' sign a little further on are for cars and not walkers. The good unmade track continues for 10mins up to the **Mas Torrat** where there are often noisy but timid dogs. Here

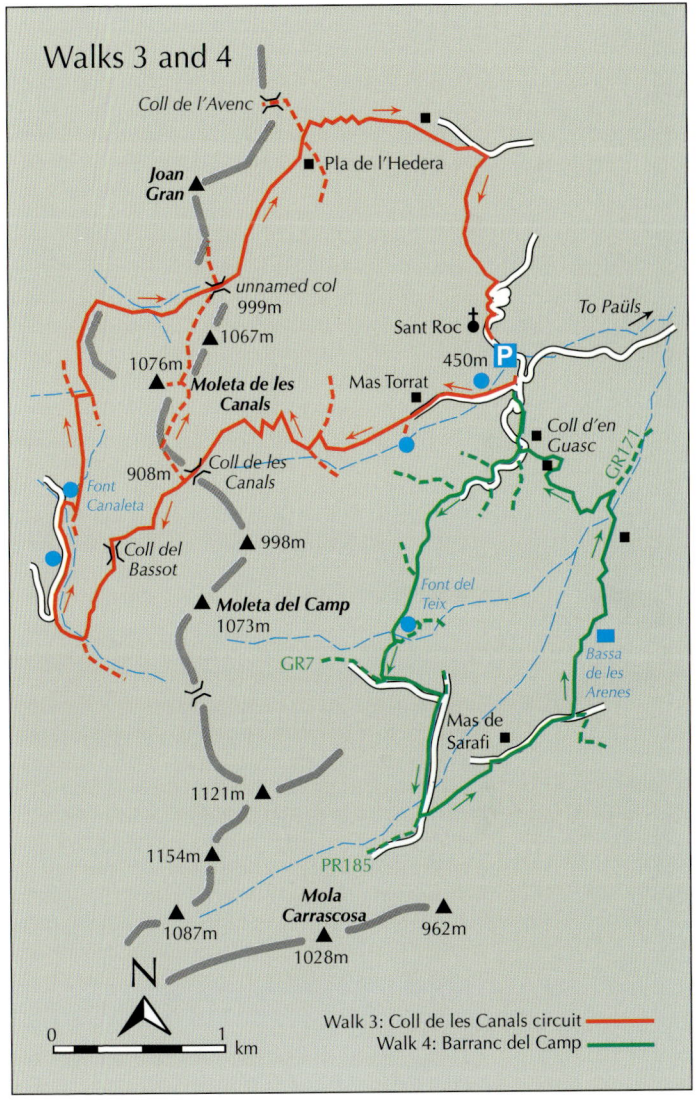

Walks 3 and 4

Coll de l'Avenc

Joan
Gran

Pla de l'Hedera

unnamed col
999m

▲1067m

1076m
▲

Moleta de les
Canals

Sant Roc

450m

Mas Torrat

Coll d'en
Guasc

GR171

908m

Coll de les
Canals

Font
Canaleta

Coll del
Bassot

▲ 998m

Moleta del Camp
1073m

Font del
Teix

GR7

Bassa
de les
Arenes

Mas de
Sarafi

1121m ▲

1154m ▲

PR185

Mola
Carrascosa

▲
1087m

▲
1028m

▲ 962m

To Paüls

N

0   1
|___|___|___|___|___| km

Walk 3: Coll de les Canals circuit ———
Walk 4: Barranc del Camp ———

the track ends at a junction of three paths. Take the right-hand path to reach the next junction 2mins later. Another right turn begins a climb on a delightful path up through the trees.

About 30mins from the start of the walk the path reaches a T-junction, marked clearly as such with red paint on a rock. Take the left turn towards the cliffs and, after 150m, make an acute right turn (marked with a cairn) to climb a narrow path, overgrown by bushes in places. The path first trends right and then zigzags up the hillside to the right of the Barranc de les Canals to reach a false col some 30mins from the T-junction. The **Coll de les Canals** is 5mins further on, over some open scree slopes. At the col the landscape changes dramatically from Mediterranean hillside to sub-alpine forest. ◄ The alternative route along the ridge starts from this col – see below.

Steep mountainsides clothed in tall pines frame the sculptural forms of the Roques Benet ahead.

To continue the circuit, descend leftwards from the col on a clear path, at first stony and steep but soon zig-zagging on grass to enter woodland. After about 12mins the path begins to climb to cross a subsidiary ridge at the **Coll del Bassot**. Here the path bears left to descend and join a grassy track some 15mins later. A right turn leads down into the main valley to meet a wide well-made track looping the edge of old pastures. Turn right again, to continue parallel to the course of the stream in the valley bottom, with magnificent steep cliffs, crowned with pine trees, rising to the right.

The track leads past the stone drinking troughs of the Font de Carrasca and then, some 45mins from the Coll de les Canals, loops to cross the stream. Look for a small path to the right which leads up to and past the **Font Canaleta** – marked as such in stone. Beyond the font the path becomes overgrown but continues for 2mins to an acute left turn with a joining path, indicated by an old yellow marker. From here this path climbs steadily, crossing a *barranc* and following occasional yellow markers.

After 15mins or so of steep climbing, the path levels out to cross a second barranc, which can be seen

dropping steeply down to the left and rising to the right as a more shallow gully. At this point a barrier of small stones across the path indicates a junction. Up to the right, cairns mark a trace of a path leading directly uphill towards the foot of the cliffs of Moleta de les Canals. This vague path practically disappears, but continue uphill for 6mins following the line of the gully to reach a cairned junction with a more obvious upper path. Turn left onto this path and continue rising towards the gap to the left of the cliff, with stunning views to the left and towering cliffs up to the right.

The path makes its way past a rocky outcrop and then climbs clearly towards a pine tree which marks a col on a subsidiary ridge, reached 10mins or so after joining the cairned path. Turning right here, the path climbs up a rocky ramp and continues rising to cross a shoulder and converge with the line of the barranc below to the left, dropping into it 7mins from the col. Turn right to follow the bed of this barranc for 20m before making a left turn into a subsidiary barranc and following a well-cairned path which rises through the

Near the Font de Carrasca on the circuit route

pine trees to the right of this shallow grassy valley. After 6mins an unnamed col with a 'Reserva Nacional de Caça' sign is reached.

From the unnamed col it is possible to make a detour to the summit of **Joan Gran**, to gain an excellent panorama. A path to the left leads up, increasingly steeply, to a ridge. Turn right along the ridge to reach a subsidiary summit after a few minutes and that of Joan Gran a few minutes later. Return by the same route. ◄

This summit detour takes about 30mins and involves 80m of ascent.

The circuit continues by crossing the unnamed col and dropping, steeply at first, through the pines. Carry straight on when a path joins from the right. Some 10mins from the col the path descends to a stone animal shelter and a junction with a broad path at the **Pla de l'Hedera**. Turning left onto this path begins a comfortable zigzag descent which arrives at a ruined building after 20mins or so. From here the path descends more steeply for 10mins and then drops onto a track. Turn right here and after 30m turn right again to find a narrow grassy track leading from a broad, flattened area. After a few minutes the track ends at a point marked by a cairn and the route continues as a

The Roques Benet from the top of Joan Gran

small path. This path undulates up and down, always in the same direction, before climbing to cross a low ridge and then dropping down to join a narrow road. Turn right onto the road and follow it down past the **Sant Roc** chapel and springs to return to the start some 1hr 20mins from the unnamed col.

Summit ridge route

Follow the Circuit route to climb up to the Coll de les Canals. Just after the col there is a rock on the right marked with old black and red paint and alongside it there is a trace of a path leading up the ridge to the right. There are no waymarks or cairns so it is necessary to find the easiest way to ascend the rocks directly. After a few minutes the rock gives way to consolidated scree interspersed with limestone pavement. The ridge is broad and can be tackled by any number of lines heading generally towards the most visible highest ground. Stay above and to the right of a shallow barranc with a 'Reserva Nacional de Caça' sign on its left and ascend through an area of bushes and low trees, heading towards a band of rock which guards the summit of the Moleta. After reaching the rock band, about 30mins from the col, contour round to the right for 5mins or so until an obvious route upwards becomes clear. Use this break in the cliffs to climb up towards a spreading pine tree where there is a small concrete boundary post and a 'Reserva Nacional de Caça' sign. From here it is an easy matter to walk up the rounded summit of the **Moleta de les Canals** and enjoy a dramatic 360° panorama of the northern els Ports massif. ▶

The summit is reached some 40mins from the Coll de les Canals.

Looking onwards along the ridge a sharply profiled peak with steep cliffs on its left side can be seen, separated from the Moleta by a dip. Descend towards it using a shallow gully and turn left into the steeper gully just below the dip. Across the gully there is a faint path running parallel with the base of the cliffs and through pine woodland. After a few minutes it becomes apparent that there are a number of contouring paths, all leading in the same direction – these are made by ibex and any can be used. Once you reach the end of the line of cliff, slant downhill to arrive at the unnamed col, approximately 15mins from the summit of the Moleta. From here follow the descent for the Circuit route.

SANT ROC

The chapel, springs and picnic site of Sant Roc are 2km to the south-west of Paüls. The water here is abundant, flowing from 16 fountain heads and the area is shaded by tall and ancient trees, including cypress, pines, maples and Mediterranean oaks. The current chapel was built in the 18th century and is dedicated to Sant Roc or Roch, patron saint of healing and of dogs. A small plaque above the spring shows the saint mysteriously exposing a wound on his knee and a dog gazing up at him. The story goes that St. Roc was born in 1295 in Montpellier, France with a curious red cross marked on his chest. At the age of 20 he gave all his wealth to the poor and travelled as a pilgrim to Italy, where many villages were suffering from the Plague. He discovered he had the power to cure the villagers and their animals alike but succumbed, eventually, to the Plague himself and went into the woods to die. There he was found by a dog that licked his wounds and brought him food, gradually restoring him to health.

With the sound of running water and the shade from the towering ancient trees it is not surprising that the people of Paüls have venerated the site over the centuries. Each year on the 16 August they celebrate the festival of Sant Roc, but they also use the site throughout the summer for picnics and barbecues and have built terraces of rostadors or corros, stone picnic tables and benches, to do this in style.

WALK 4

Barranc del Camp

Difficulty	Route-finding ● Scrambling ● Exposure ●
Total ascent	370m
Time	2hrs
Distance	10km
Start	Ermita de Sant Roc
Maps	Either Estels del Sud, Editorial Piolet, 1:25,000 (preferred) or El Port Nord, Editorial Piolet, 1:30,000 For route map, see Walk 3.

For full directions to start, see Appendix B.

The broad valleys extending up from Paüls to above Sant Roc are a maze of footpaths and tracks among woodland and small farms of olive, almond and cherry. This easy excursion explores two valleys above Sant Roc: the Barranc del Camp and the Barranc del Salt. These valleys are bounded on both sides by steep cliffs and separated in their upper reaches by a huge buttress. The route makes use of three well-marked footpaths and links them with farm tracks (many junctions but all are clear) to form a circular walk. The walk is delightful on a warm spring day when the fruit trees are in blossom and it is a good option when there are strong winds on the high ridges.

Leave the area of **Sant Roc** along the track which is waymarked in red and white (GR7) and blue (Estels del Sud). After 100m the waymarks indicate a path to the left which makes a shortcut and rejoins the main track 5mins later, just below the **Coll d'en Guasc**. From here the track winds steadily up through pine and holly oak woods and narrows to become a footpath. Ignore paths leading left or right and stay with the red and white and the blue waymarks.

After 20mins the path climbs to a junction where another path joins acutely from the right. Continue

It is well worth a short detour to this picturesque spot with its ancient stonework and wooden log conduits.

straight on downhill to arrive, 8mins or so later, at a fork with no obvious markers. Taking the right branch a red and white marker confirms the direction some 50m further on. A few minutes later the path descends to cross a *barranc* and reach a junction. The path dropping down to the left leads to the **Font del Teix** 50m below. ◄

Having visited the *font*, return to the GR7/Estels footpath and climb steeply for 8mins or so to join a broad well-made track at a T-junction. Leave the GR7/Estels path here and turn left along the track, reaching a junction with another track 5mins later. Turn right onto this track which now curves close around the huge buttress dividing the two valleys before heading into the Barranc del Salt. After 10mins the track reaches a junction with a footpath, the PR-C185, where a yellow and white waymark can be seen on a rock to the left. Turn left onto this footpath, and the yellow and white waymarks lead on through woodland until the path drops, some 12mins later, onto a broad track.

Turning right, the track passes the ruins of the **Mas de Sarafi** and continues for a further 10mins or so to a

Almond blossom in March below the Montaspre ridge

signposted crossroads with the red and white waymarked GR171 footpath. Turn left onto the GR171, down past a ruined building to an impressive water reservoir, the **Bassa de les Arenes**, which provides both drinking and irrigation water for the farms in the valley below. Just after the Bassa the footpath converges with a track. Continue straight on into an area of well-tended olive and almond terraces and small farms, descending to ford a stream and reach a junction of tracks. Turn right here and after a short distance the track becomes a surfaced road.

About 2mins after crossing the stream there is junction with a concrete-surfaced track which joins acutely from the left. Turn left onto this to leave the GR171 and climb up the concreted section until it becomes an unsurfaced track. At this point a cairn marks a junction. Bear right onto a rougher track and continue rising by a terrace wall for 4mins until another rough track joins from the left. Continue straight on past a 'No entry' sign and pass by the side of a chain barring vehicular traffic. The path now becomes grassy underfoot and curves around the base of a drystone wall, before becoming stony and winding up towards an old farm building with a well-preserved stone water cistern.

By the building an acute right turn leads past another chain onto a rising track which climbs up to reach a crossroads with a ruined building to the right. This is the **Coll d'en Guasc** where the circuit is completed and a right turn rejoins the GR7/Estels footpath. Continue for about 20m before turning right again onto the shortcut path and following the waymarks down to return to **Sant Roc**.

WALK 5
Solana route

Difficulty	Route-finding ●● Scrambling ●● Exposure ●●
Total ascent	700m
Time	4hrs 15mins
Distance	14km
Start	el Toscar
Maps	Either Estels del Sud, Editorial Piolet, 1:25,000 (preferred) or El Port Nord, Editorial Piolet, 1:30,000

For full directions to start, see Appendix B.

This is an exhilarating walk for those who enjoy high balcony routes and are confident on steep and stony terrain. The route is on clear paths up to the Cova dels Adells, along the ridge and for the descent, but there is a section after the Mas del Roig where the route has to be chosen with care to gain the ridge. This balcony section offers spectacular views of Mont Caro, the steep cliffs dropping below to the el Toscar valley, the broad Ebre valley, Tortosa and the Mediterranean beyond. Once the ridge is reached the dramatic contrasts between the eastern and western sides of els Ports can be seen as the path hugs the rocky ridge for a while before descending into deep woodland on the western side and then returning to el Toscar via the Coll de Carabasses down a good path. (For more information on els Ports see Walk 16.)

In the spring purple and white anemones, wood violets and cowslips line the sides of the path.

Take the right path at the signpost by the electricity sub-station for the Cova dels Adells and turn right again at the first junction reached 1min later. Follow the path, with red markers, for another 10mins to reach another signpost. Continue straight on, again for the Cova dels Adells. After a stony start, the path passes more gently through a woodland area where red squirrels can sometimes be seen among the holly oaks and pines. ◄ A third signpost, 5mins from the last, indicates a path to the

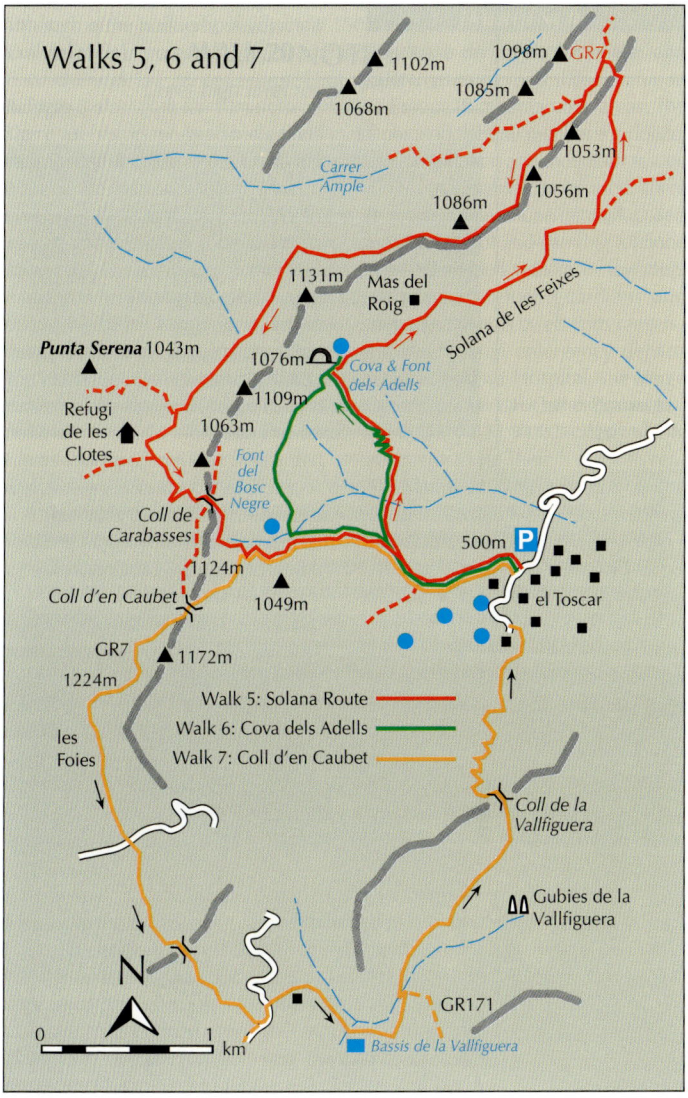

Walks 5, 6 and 7

1102m
1068m
1098m
1085m
GR7
1053m
1056m
Carrer Ample
1086m
1131m
Mas del Roig
Solana de les Feixes
Punta Serena 1043m
1076m
Cova & Font dels Adells
1109m
Refugi de les Clotes
1063m
Font del Bosc Negre
Coll de Carabasses
1124m
500m
P
el Toscar
Coll d'en Caubet
1049m
GR7
1172m
1224m
les Foies
Coll de la Vallfiguera
Gubies de la Vallfiguera

Walk 5: Solana Route
Walk 6: Cova dels Adells
Walk 7: Coll d'en Caubet

N

GR171

0   1 km

Bassis de la Vallfiguera

Coll de Carabasses to the left (used on the descent) and the onward route, signed for the Cova, to the right. The onward path passes a ruined *mas* after a few metres and reaches the (signposted) Barranc de Bosc Negre after further 7mins. The path now begins to climb, offering views to the right across the tops of the woodlands to the ridges beyond.

About 30mins from the start, the path reaches a gate with a sign warning of *Bous Braus*, wild bulls. Pass through the gate and follow the path across a minor *barranc* before zigzagging up the open stony hillside opposite. The path then briefly re-enters woodland before emerging high on the left-hand side of a valley which drops down to el Toscar as a narrow gorge. The landscape now becomes more open and arid-looking as you reach the (signposted) **Cova dels Adells**, 40mins from the start.

Just past the cave a yellow waymark indicates the way forward on a narrow path which rises close to the rock wall. After passing a second cave and the **Font dels Adells** the path rises diagonally towards some drystone terrace walls which can be seen above. Pass through a

Looking back at the Cova dels Adells

breach in the first wall, turn right and follow the grassy terrace to its end. Here a cairn indicates a narrow path leading on through box bushes and across a shallow barranc. The now stony path rises on the opposite side of the barranc, crosses a rickety fence and then descends a little before rising again to pass by a rocky outcrop.

From here the path becomes a little indistinct but it climbs up by the left-hand side of some terrace walls to the top of a small rise and passes onto a flatter area. After crossing this and rounding a corner, pass below some more terrace walls before rising diagonally across an area of inclined limestone pavement, to reach a notch on the low rise ahead. The path now climbs diagonally left towards some undercut cliffs which shelter the ruins of the **Mas del Roig**, reached some 17mins from the Cova dels Adells.

After the Mas del Roig, follow the main terrace which crosses a minor barranc and then turn left onto a stony path that climbs diagonally, passing through bushes to gain the shoulder ahead. From here the path descends on scree to cross the next barranc and then rises to pass to the left of the lowest point of the next col, and continues to rise. ▶ Continue to reach a rocky step down, where the path appears to be blocked by a fence. Pass round the right-hand end of the fence and drop down across scree to gain another path which can be seen below. Looking back, it can be seen that this path has its origin at a cave under the rocky step.

Here there are fine views across the valley below to the sea in the distance.

Some 20mins from the Mas del Roig the path crosses the head of a narrow, subsidiary valley which is overshadowed by steep cliffs. ▶ After rounding the next corner the trace of the path can be seen ahead, rising diagonally up the hillside (to the north-east). Continue on this path, keeping the direction for approximately 20mins to a point where some steep zigzags can be discerned to the left, rising more directly up towards the ridge. Follow these onto a small grassy plateau and from here the main ridge is easily gained, about an hour from the Mas del Roig. Due to the lack of definite landmarks it is possible to overshoot the zigzags. If so, the path leads on to a

Down below can be seen a bull farm, with its bullring and some reservoirs.

November afternoon sun creates dramatic shadows on the Solana ridge

scree-filled gully, which should not be crossed. Instead, ascend the hillside to the left of the gully and then go to the left of the buttress above to gain the main ridge.

There is a clear footpath across the ridge, marked in red and white for the GR7 and blue for the Estels route. Turn left onto this to walk along the ridge, with dramatic views on both sides. Some 30mins after gaining the ridge the path drops definitively to the right-hand side of the ridge (clearly marked with red and white markers) and, soon after, plunges into woodland. After the initial descent, the path undulates through the woodland, until 12mins later, at a sharp left turn, it starts to descend decisively. At this turn there is a faint path leading right for about 30m to a viewpoint, from which the Mas de la Franqueta and the valley of the Riu dels Estrets can be seen far below. The path now winds downhill to reach flatter ground and comes to a forest glade with the newly renovated (unguarded and unlocked) **Refugi de les Clotes**, some 45mins after entering the woodland.

The waymarked path (red and white and blue) now turns a right-angle to the left to leave the glade and emerge from the woods, 10mins later, in a rocky basin. The **Coll de Carabasses** and its trig point can be seen ahead. The col is reached in 2mins; crossing it, leave the GR7/Estels path and bear right to descend on a stony path which takes a steepish zigzag way down. Several stony gullies appear to be shortcuts for the zigzags, but mostly they are not. ▶ Some 7mins after starting the descent the path crosses a dry barranc and stays level for a short while before reaching a junction with a small metal signpost plate which indicates left for el Toscar. Continue with the descending zigzags for a further 35mins until a signpost points right for el Toscar. Another signpost appears 12mins later and marks the end of the circuit. Turn right for el Toscar to reach the start after a further 14mins or so.

Occasional red markers and cairns help to guide the descent.

EL TOSCAR AND THE VALLCERVERA

The Toscar and Cervera valleys lie side by side, separated by a ridge and surrounded by the higher mountains of els Ports. Vallcervera is now a region of deserted pastures and small farm ruins, while the Toscar valley has a hamlet of summer and weekend houses and a restaurant (summer opening only) at the end of the road. About 1km before el Toscar there are some dramatic ruins, perched on rocky outcrops. These are the remains of the ancient settlement of Carles, which was abandoned in 1479 because of Plague. It is now reduced to the ruined fortifications of a once substantial castle plus the restored parish church of Sant Julia, to which there is a pilgrimage procession each Easter.

WALK 6
Cova dels Adells

Difficulty	Route-finding ● Scrambling ● Exposure ●
Total ascent	325m
Time	1hr 25mins
Distance	5km
Start	el Toscar
Maps	Either Estels del Sud, Editorial Piolet, 1:25,000 (preferred) or El Port Nord, Editorial Piolet, 1:30,000 For route map, see Walk 5.

For full directions to start, see Appendix B.

This gentle and well-signposted circular walk takes the same route as Walk 5 up to the open limestone hillsides surrounding the Cova dels Adells, but returns through woodland via the deep mossy shade of the Font del Bosc Negre (the spring of the black wood).

Follow the route description for Walk 5, The Solana route, as far as the **Cova dels Adells** which is reached some 40mins from the car park.

Having visited the cave, return to the signpost and bear right in the direction of the Font del Bosc Negre. The yellow waymarked path rises gently to cross a flat grassy area and then descends towards a gate, which is reached 5mins after leaving the Cova dels Adells. A signpost requests, in Catalan, that you close the gate behind you. After descending steeply, the path undulates up and down through woodland to reach the Font del Bosc Negre some 15mins later. Cliffs, romantically overgrown with ivy and mosses, and a handsome old stone trough make this a special place.

Just 2mins after leaving the font the path joins a major footpath at a signposted junction. Carry straight on in the direction signposted to el Toscar for a further 12mins to reach another junction which completes the circuit. Turn right here for el Toscar and arrive back at the start some 14mins later.

The landscape becomes more arid approaching the Cova dels Adells

WALK 7
Coll d'en Caubet and Vallfiguera

Difficulty	Route-finding ●● Scrambling ● Exposure ●
Total ascent	850m
Time	4hrs 15mins
Distance	12km
Start	el Toscar
Maps	Either Estels del Sud, Editorial Piolet, 1:25,000 (preferred) or El Port Nord, Editorial Piolet, 1:30,000 For route map, see Walk 5.

For full directions to start, see Appendix B.

Variety is the hallmark of this walk, which takes advantage of some little used footpaths to link two long-distance routes and so create a circular walk of interest and diversity. An ascent by crags and through steep woodland leads onto almost flat pastureland above the main ridge. These are the Foies, shallow but broad depressions amidst rocks, where moisture is trapped enabling grass to flourish. Later, a little-used path gives access to a dramatic and hidden valley at the head of a pinnacle-guarded ravine.

Take the right-hand path at the signpost by the electricity sub-station for the Cova dels Adells and the Coll de Carabasses and turn right at the first junction, reached a minute later. Follow the red markers to another signpost, after 10mins, pointing onwards for the Cova dels Adells. At a third signpost, 5mins later, take a left turn for the Coll de Carabasses (2.8km) and continue following the red markers to climb through woodland to another signposted junction. Again make a left turn towards the Coll de Carabasses (2km) and continue climbing on a well-used path. Just over an hour from the start of the walk the route diverges left onto a narrower path. The junction is marked with the word 'Clotes' in red paint on a rock, over which there is a small metal plate, indicating the left turn for the Coll d'en Caubet and les Foies.

The path is now unmarked and overgrown in some places by box bushes, which are easily pushed aside. After 10mins the path crosses a low ridge (not the col itself) and bears to the right to continue climbing. After passing a cairned path leading down to the left, a small band of rocks comes into view on the right. The route climbs to the right-hand side of this rockband before bearing left to cross over the top.

Having left the rocks, the cairned path climbs into a more tree-covered area with pine needles underfoot. About 5mins later box bushes all but obscure the route, but pushing through them quickly reveals a clearer path and a cairn. A few minutes later the path emerges onto an open rocky hillside and zigzags up to reach the **Coll d'en Caubet** after some 5mins. Here the route joins the combined path of the GR7 (red and white waymarks) and the Estels route (blue waymarks).

Turn left along the now very obvious path to climb up to the highest point of the walk, reached

The pastures of les Foies

approximately 1hr 45mins from the start. This unnamed hill overlooks les Foies, a surprising landscape of animal pasture, enclosures and farm buildings. ◄ Red and white GR7 markers lead down across the **les Foies** pastures, to enter woodland and descend to a track reached some 15mins from the highest point. Follow the red and white markers across the track to continue straight on, on a comfortable broad grassy track. After 10mins the way-marks lead off the track to the right and a small path begins to climb quite steeply for a few minutes before making a steep rocky descent to reach a second track some 25mins later.

Turn left onto this track and go past a building and a sign board, 'Cami de les Foies', both on the right. Also, on the right here, there is a stone wall made of large blocks of dressed and carved stone, clearly taken from some previously important building. Where the dressed stone finishes and the rough stone starts there is a small gap with a faded yellow paint mark. This is the start of the route towards the head of the Vallfiguera.

Leave the track and pass through the wall where traces of two paths can be made out in the grass. Take the right, less obvious of these to find a building and a mast with a solar panel. Pass to the left of the building and look for a series of small cairns which lead the way down to a small rocky clearing. The path, marked by a cairn, descends to the right from here, becoming much clearer as it enters pine trees and begins its traverse along the right-hand side of an ever-steepening valley. Rocky cliffs, ridges and escarpments rise on both sides as the path enters the dramatic and sculptured landscape at the head of the Vallfiguera.

Some 20mins after leaving the track the path crosses the dry floor of the *barranc* for the first time and continues on for 10mins to reach a water trough. This is the **Bassis de la Vall de la Figuera**. After a further 5mins cross the barranc for a second time. This time the path turns left into the dry riverbed and then turns immediately right by a cairn and a red and white marker to join the GR171 route. This path climbs away from the barranc

Here the traditional black bulls of the area can usually be seen roaming freely.

Looking down into the Vallfiguera

to negotiate the steep ridges, cliffs and pinnacles which characterise the terrain between the Vallfiguera and the Toscar valley. It then levels somewhat before climbing once more to cross the **Coll de la Vallfiguera**.

After this the path crosses some subsidiary ridges before descending finally in a series of zigzags. Some 1hr 10mins after joining the GR171 the path reaches el Toscar. Turn left onto the road to pass the many springs for which el Toscar is known, and pass the chapel of Santa Magdalena before bearing right at the next junction to return to the start a few minutes later.

WALK 8
Cervera and Figuera valleys

Difficulty	Route-finding ● Scrambling ● (●●● for the Vallfiguera) Exposure ●
Total ascent	270m plus 225m for the Vallfiguera
Time	2hrs 30mins plus 2hrs 30mins for the Vallfiguera
Distance	10km plus 5km for the Vallfiguera
Start	la Peixera de la Flor
Maps	Either Estels del Sud, Editorial Piolet, 1:25,000 (preferred) or El Port Nord, Editorial Piolet, 1:30,000

For full directions to start, see Appendix B.

This is a gentle circular walk in the pastoral Cervera valley, with its low waterfalls, natural rock pools and picturesque abandoned farms, overlooked by the crags of the Caro massif. At the furthest point of this walk, confident scramblers can extend the route with a 'there and back' climb up the spectacular Vallfiguera – the valley of the fig tree. This ends in the *Gubies*, a narrow passage cut by the river through the towering cliffs that guard the head of the valley.

Continue along the road, which soon becomes a track, and pass a rabbit farm with noisy but safely fenced dogs. From here the track rises and comes to a junction with a concrete road. Turning left, this descends to a ford across the river. Just before the ford a chained track leads off to the right. Pass the chain and take this track to continue with the river on the left and some low cliffs on the right. The track soon becomes grassy and passes an old caravan where it bears left to cross a small olive grove and follow a terrace wall. A few minutes later the now faint path leaves the terrace wall to cross a new olive plantation and reach the true left bank of the river. A white waymark confirms the route.

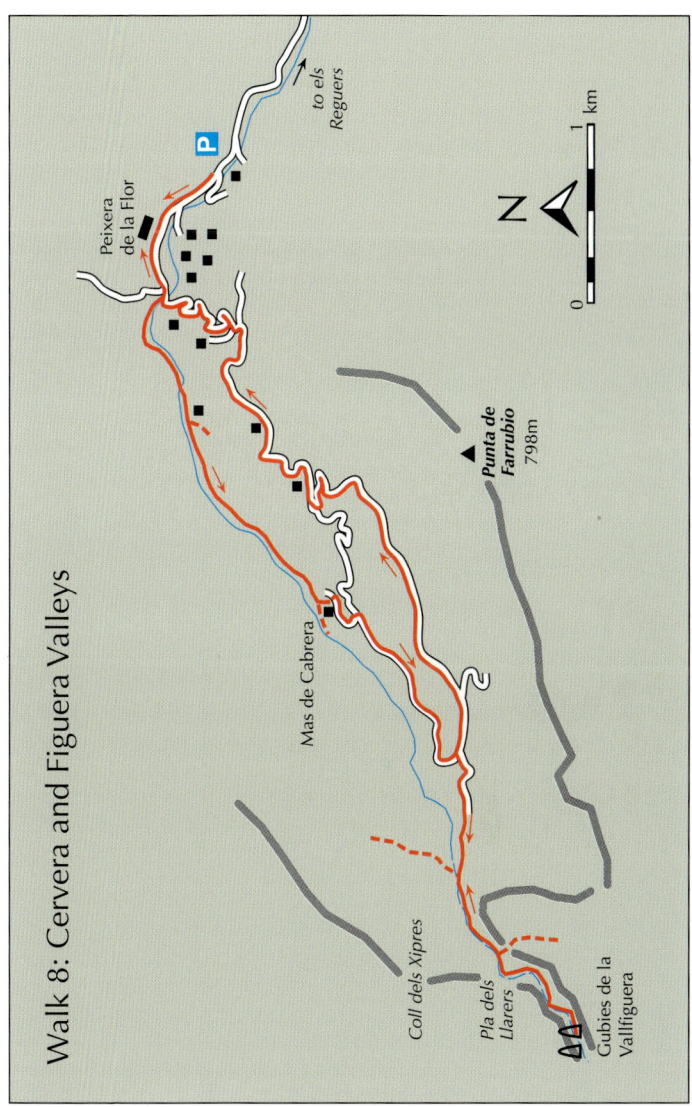

Walk 8: Cervera and Figuera Valleys

to els Reguers

Peixera de la Flor

Punta de Farrubio
798m

Mas de Cabrera

Coll dels Xipres

Pla dels Llarers

Gubies de la Vallfiguera

1 km

0

N

Some 20mins from the start the path climbs through an old terrace wall and a couple of minutes later, a red waymark indicates a left turn into the dry riverbed. After following the riverbed for 50m another red marker leads out onto a path leading upriver on the opposite bank, passing through an olive and almond grove. Some five minutes later the path passes to the right of two ruined buildings. Immediately after the second building the path forks; ignore the left turn, which is waymarked in red, and fork right to join a narrow irrigation channel a minute later and continue on a path alongside it. After 10mins cross the channel to find a continuation path to the right, leading under some overhanging cliffs with small caves and the remains of an animal shelter. From here the path climbs up above the river, passes through a makeshift gate and comes to an area of grassy terraces.

Carry straight on across the terrace to an orange waymark on the boundary wall to the left. From here the path climbs up the terraces, bearing right and then left with orange markers confirming the route, to emerge at a grove of old olive trees. Continue across in the line of the valley to find an orange waymark and a cairn which lead leftwards to a path that winds up to another terrace. Follow the terrace wall, leading to the large ruined **Mas de Cabrera**, reached some 15mins after the overhanging cliffs. Some stone steps up to the left by the *mas* indicate the continuation of the route. ◀ However, to visit the waterfalls pass to the right of the *mas* and under a huge Mediterranean oak to cross a broken-down fence and then turn right off the path to reach the river. Retrace the route back to the *mas* to resume the walk.

Climb the steps to find a clear track leading up and away from the river. After 4mins turn right at a T-junction; the scenery soon opens out to give extensive views of the cliffs of the Tossa de la Reina up to the left. ◀ After 20mins a second T-junction is reached, where a right turn is marked by a cairn. At this point turn left to continue the circuit, or turn right to start the Vallfiguera extension.

A two-minute detour will take you to a pleasant spot where the river forms a series of rockpools and low waterfalls.

Up ahead, following the line of the river valley, is the first view of the Vallfiguera.

Vallfiguera extension

After 8mins or so the track comes to an end in a flat grassy area with a large central pine tree. A small clear path continues on in the same direction, climbing across an area of boulders and then up through trees. After 10mins it descends to cross a small side *barranc*, bends sharply to the left and then bends sharply right shortly afterwards to avoid entering a boulder-filled gully. Some 5mins later, cairns guide the way across a boulder field and up to a gap between rocks. Here the descent into the barranc de la Vallfiguera is made by a short, easy scramble, following cairns down to a flat shingle area with a prominent fig tree.

From here the scrambling stays intermittently difficult throughout. The course of the barranc is a maze of water-sculpted rock and huge boulders, although it remains dry in most weathers. A sloping slab provides an exit from the shingle area and some useful cairns appear shortly afterwards but route-finding remains important to avoid cul-de-sacs. After 15mins the route leaves the bed of the barranc and climbs to the right, firstly through bushes

The ruins of the Mas de Cabrera

73

and then up a boulder slope. At the top of this slope there is a red painted sign on a rock wall pointing to 'les Gubies'. From here a clear path crosses a scree slope and enters bushes, becoming overgrown but remaining quite distinct.

At 12mins from the painted sign the path re-enters the barranc and crosses it to arrive shortly at the **Pla dels Llarers**, a small clearing with a miniature metal signpost set at its centre. This signpost indicates a route left for Caro and onwards for the Gubies. Head onwards and re-enter the bed of the barranc; the path continues along it until it reaches the entrance to the **Gubies** 15mins from the Pla. It is possible to walk along the bottom of the dark, forbidding and spectacular cleft of the Gubies for some distance until a terminus is reached marked by huge chockstones, a dark pool and a series of bolts in the rock wall for a hand traverse on some old and dubious rope. Returning by the same route, the exit from the barranc is reached after 40mins and the T-junction, at which the circuit is resumed, some 25mins after that.

Returning to la Peixera de la Flor, with the Solana ridge ahead

To continue the circuit

Having turned left, continue along the track, ignoring another track to the right encountered 4mins later. After approximately 30mins the track reaches a junction and descends in a loop to a picturesque ruined *mas* surrounded by open pasture. Shortly, the track is blocked by a metal barrier which can be passed on its left-hand side. About 5mins later pass a large green gate, also on its left-hand side. ▶ At the next junction take the left track and then turn right at a second junction 50m further on, to descend in a series of loops to the river. Cross this by the ford to reach the chained entrance which marks the start of the outward route. All that remains is to negotiate the rabbit farm once more to return to the start.

The gates are barriers for livestock and vehicles, not walkers.

WALK 9
La Moleta

Difficulty	Route-finding ● Scrambling ● (●● optional) Exposure ● (●●● optional)
Total ascent	460m
Time	2hrs 20mins
Distance	6km
Start	Font Nova
Map	El Port Nord, Editorial Piolet, 1:30,000

For full directions to start, see Appendix B.

La Moleta can be seen from many directions: an impregnable fortress block that looks almost man-made. The walk starts from the Font Nova, a spring and picnic site. Well signposted footpaths circle la Moleta and there is an opportunity to reach the summit with the help of cables and rungs set into the rock. The display boards at Font Nova suggest doing this walk in an anticlockwise direction which requires a steep descent from the Moleta on a rather eroded footpath. This is much more comfortable as an ascent and a clockwise description is given here.

Leave the car park and ascend diagonally left through the springs area, following the signpost for Refugi de la Font Nova and la Moleta. Yellow and white waymarks lead up though the broken walls of old olive terraces for 5mins to the refuge (unguarded and locked). Turn left onto a broader path signposted to the Font de Domingo and pass through a wooden gate. The path weaves through trees to arrive at another signpost after a couple of minutes. Take the right turn here, signposted to the Font de Domingo and la Moleta, and follow the narrow path around various ruined buildings. ◄ The path emerges after a while into more grassy open country, climbing gently through low-growing gorse, wild lavender and rosemary. The blocky summit of la Moleta can now be seen slightly to the right as the path

This area seems particularly rich in woodland birds, although they are more easily heard than seen.

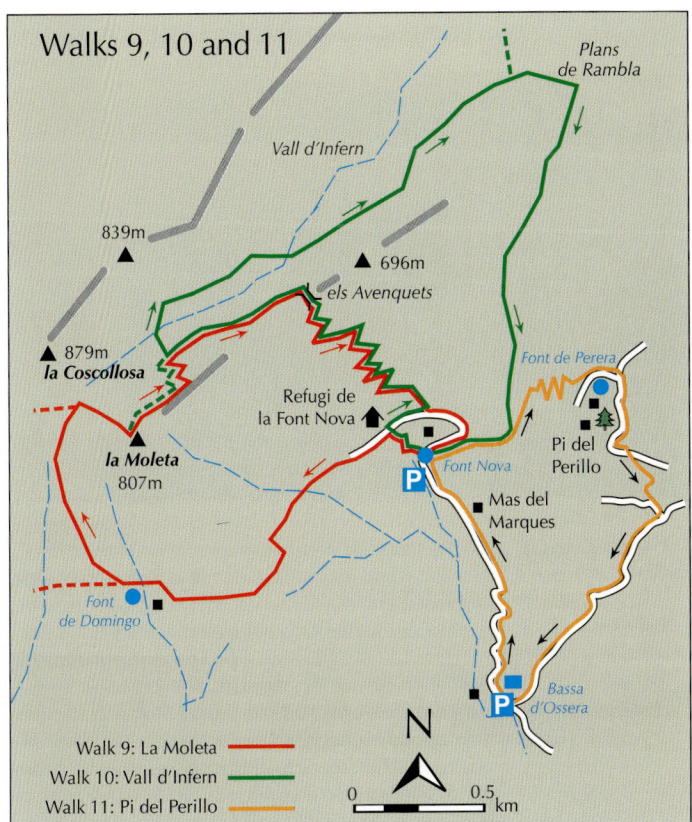

Walks 9, 10 and 11

Plans de Rambla

Vall d'Infern

839m ▲

▲ 696m

els Avenquets

▲ 879m
la Coscollosa

Font de Perera

Refugi de
la Font Nova

Pi del
Perillo

la Moleta
807m

Font Nova

Mas del
Marques

**Font
de Domingo**

Bassa
d'Ossera

N

Walk 9: La Moleta ———
Walk 10: Vall d'Infern ———
Walk 11: Pi del Perillo ———

0   0.5
└─────┴─────┘ km

circles around it, dropping towards a ruined *mas* and then veering to the right to approach the **Font de Domingo** with its animal drinking trough, spring and signpost.

The signpost indicates the direction for la Moleta (1.4km). From here the path climbs steeply up towards the summit, encountering the loose and eroded sections mentioned in the introduction. This stage ends at a signposted junction some 35mins from the Font de Domingo. Take a right turn at this junction, towards the Refugi de

Scrambling on the arête of la Moleta

la Font Nova and head directly for la Moleta on the yellow and white waymarked path. The base of **la Moleta** is reached after 5mins and yet another signpost appears, marking the start of the summit climb.

The scramble up is short and easy, thanks to cables and iron rungs set into the arête. The summit is a broad flat platform, approached across a rather exposed step. The views are fantastic across the river to the Cardó massif and down to the twin riverside villages of Xerta (right bank) and Tivenys (left bank). Just upriver is the Xerta Assut (weir), built by the Moors and restored in the 12th century. ◄

Before leaving the summit, look for the metal canister containing the visitors' book.

Reverse the climb on the arête to regain the junction of paths at its foot. A signpost points the direction for the Refugi de la Font Nova and the Font Nova on a path which follows the ridge before dropping more steeply to the left on a series of zigzags to another signposted junction. Take the right turn (Font Nova 1.9km) leading to **els Avenquets**, a small signposted col that marks the final descent to Font Nova. The refuge is reached after 30mins or so and from here it is easy to take a left turn and stroll along the broad track back to **Font Nova**.

WALK 10
Vall d'Infern

Difficulty	Route-finding ● Scrambling ● (●● extension) Exposure ● (●●● extension)
Total ascent	320m plus 140m for extension to la Moleta summit
Time	1hr 40mins plus 45mins for extension
Distance	5km plus 2km for extension
Start	Font Nova
Map	El Port Nord, Editorial Piolet, 1:30,000 For route map, see Walk 9.

For full directions to start, see Appendix B.

The varied circular walk incorporates a descent through the dramatic landscape of the 'infernal valley' and an optional there-and-back extension to climb to the summit of la Moleta (see introduction to Walk 9). The paths are obvious on the ground and very well signposted. The return path along the south-facing slopes can often be sunny and sheltered when there are strong winds on the ridge.

Leave the car park and ascend diagonally left through the springs area, following the signpost for Refugi de la Font Nova and la Moleta. Yellow and white waymarks lead up though the broken walls of old olive terraces for 5mins to the refuge (unguarded and locked). Turn right here and some 50m past the refuge turn left onto a path with yellow and white waymarks. The path weaves its way up through old terraces with several changes of direction but is always obvious on the ground and clearly waymarked in yellow and white.

Leaving the terraces behind, it enters a more open, rocky landscape and reaches the col at **els Avenquets** on the ridge some half an hour from the start. The signpost on the col points to the left to la Moleta; take this path and continue ascending around the hill before dropping down to another signpost 7mins or so later. Here there is a choice to make a 45min extension to climb to the summit of la Moleta or to take the right turn and continue with the circuit.

To climb la Moleta turn left (signposted la Moleta 900m) on a path which zigzags steeply up to a broad ridge. From here a gentle climb leads to the base of the **la Moleta** cliff, where a signpost indicates the assisted climb up the arête to the summit (traversed in reverse in Walk 9). Return by the same route to rejoin the circuit at the signpost.

To continue the circuit take the turn signposted 'Font de la Vall d'Infern 1.4km' to cross a small *barranc* and bear to the right. It is not waymarked but it is clear on the ground and cairned. The cairns lead down to the rocky entrance at the head of the **Vall de l'Infern** and on to a steep descent. As the incline eases near a boulder slope keep to the right-hand side of the valley, leaving the rocky

Looking along the line of the path, high above the Vall d'Infern

area by a marker post with a red triangle. Ignore a path to the left, marked with a cairn. The path winds below rocky ridges, sculptured pinnacles and twisted pine trees to find its way over the tops of precipitous cliffs on the valley's right-hand side.

About 30mins after leaving the col at els Avenquets (not including the summit detour!), the path begins to descend down a stony area and comes to a junction marked with a cairn. The left and steeper branch is, in fact, simply a shortcut. Keep straight on to make a wide zigzag down to a marker post (red diamond) where the shortcut also ends. From here the route contours to reach the Font de la Vall d'Infern some 5mins later.

From the font the path climbs to enter an area of pine trees and shortly reaches a signposted junction. Bear right for the **Plans de Rambla** (600m) and the Font Nova (2km) and begin crossing a broad ridge. Another signpost confirms the direction and the path now winds through low bushes and pine trees which cover the Plans de Rambla. It then emerges into more open country and climbs to a small rise which marks the end of the ridge crossing. From here a descending path crosses the sheltered south-facing slopes (*solana*) with wide open views of the broad Ebre valley and the Delta beyond. Some 20mins after crossing the ridge a signpost confirms the direction for Font Nova (500m). The path soon joins a track where a left turn leads down to the start.

WALK 11

Pi del Perillo

Difficulty	Route-finding ● Scrambling ● Exposure ●
Total ascent	140m
Time	1hr 20mins
Distance	5km
Start	Bassa d'Ossera
Map	No map available but very well signposted
	For route map, see Walk 9.

For full directions to start, see Appendix B.

This easy, well-signposted walk is a good option when there are strong winds on the high ridges. For the most part it crosses south-facing slopes or *solana*, which are terraced with dry stone walls and planted with venerable olive trees, although nature is now reclaiming the terraces. It is a walk rich in reminders of the traditional rural way of life that persisted here until the second half of the last century. Numerous small farmhouses dot the landscape, some in ruins but some restored and clearly still in use. The focal point of the walk is the Pi del Perillo, a monumental white pine, protected and preserved by the Catalan Department of the Environment.

The twin villages of Xerta and Tivenys straddle the Ebre river immediately below, with the dark ridges of the Serra de Cardó rising beyond them.

Leave the car and continue on the road towards the Font Nova on foot. After approximately 1.5km the road passes the grand but ruined **Mas del Marques** and then terminates at the car park and picnic site at the **Font Nova** springs. At this point look for a stony track leading off to the right, signposted to the Font de Perera and the Font de la Vall d'Infern, which has yellow waymarks. Follow this track for a minute or so to a second signpost and turn right here onto a short section of loose stony path (still with yellow waymarks) to reach the highest point of the walk 7mins later. This small col reveals a superb view of the river meandering out through the Delta to the sea beyond. ◀

Here a signpost for Font de Perera (1.2km) points to a narrow path to the right which zigzags down and diagonally across the terraced hillside for 10mins to reach another signpost by the side of a ruined building. The signpost points the way onward to the Font de Perera (650m) and the Pi del Perillo. About 5mins later the path converges with a track and a left turn leads quickly down to the **Font de Perera**, with its small house (*casita*) and giant stone picnic tables.

Take the stony track, signposted to the Pi del Perillo, which passes down below the house and on past another *casita* to reach the **Pi del Perillo** some 10mins later. This huge, spreading and venerable tree now dwarfs the *casita* it was intended to shade.

The route for the Bassa d'Ossera (1.6km) is not straight on as the signpost just before the Pi de Perillo seems to indicate. It actually makes a right-angle turn to the right, to pass beneath the tree and round the corner of the building onto a track. About 50m further on a second misleading signpost (Bassa d'Ossera) fails to indicate a small but well-used path leading down to the right, which is in fact the correct route. The junction is marked with a cairn. After 7mins or so the path reaches an unsignposted T-junction. Turn left onto the broader track to reach a second T-junction shortly after, where a signpost confirms a right turn for the Bassa d'Ossera (1.2km). Continue on this broad track which leads directly to the car park at the **Bassa d'Ossera**. ▶

Look out for an old limekiln on the right and partially hidden by a pine tree, about 15mins after the last T-junction.

Font de Perera

WALK 12
Mont Caro summit

Difficulty	Route-finding ●●● Scrambling ●●● Exposure ●●
Total ascent	650m
Time	3hrs 30mins
Distance	7km
Start	Coll del Vicari on Mont Caro
Maps	Either Estels del Sud, Editorial Piolet, 1:25,000 (preferred) or El Port Nord, Editorial Piolet, 1:30,000

Note The maps provide general guidance but do not reflect the complex topography or footpath routes of this area accurately.

For full directions to start, see Appendix B.

This circular walk gives access to the steep, dramatic country high up on the eastern-facing slopes and ridges of els Ports. Sustained attention to route finding is needed and there are frequent scrambling sections, although none is difficult. A switchback route leads across rocky slabs, buttresses and wooded terraces below the Caro summit before climbing to a col and finding a way up the steep summit ridge. The views from the ridge and summit are spectacular. It is said that, on a very clear day, even Mallorca can be seen – with binoculars. The route passes two historic features: the Forn de la Pimpollada, a restored 'oven' or kiln built into the hillside and formerly used to render pitch from the pine trees close by for ship-building down on the coast; and lo Comptador (the 'counter' or 'meter' in English), so-called because this narrow passage between two pinnacles was used by shepherds to count their animals through one by one. (For more information on els Ports see Walk 16.)

The walk starts approximately 150m beyond the **Coll del Vicari**, at a green signpost marked 'els Bassis de Caro 1hr' and 'la Caramella 3hrs'. Drop down from the road on

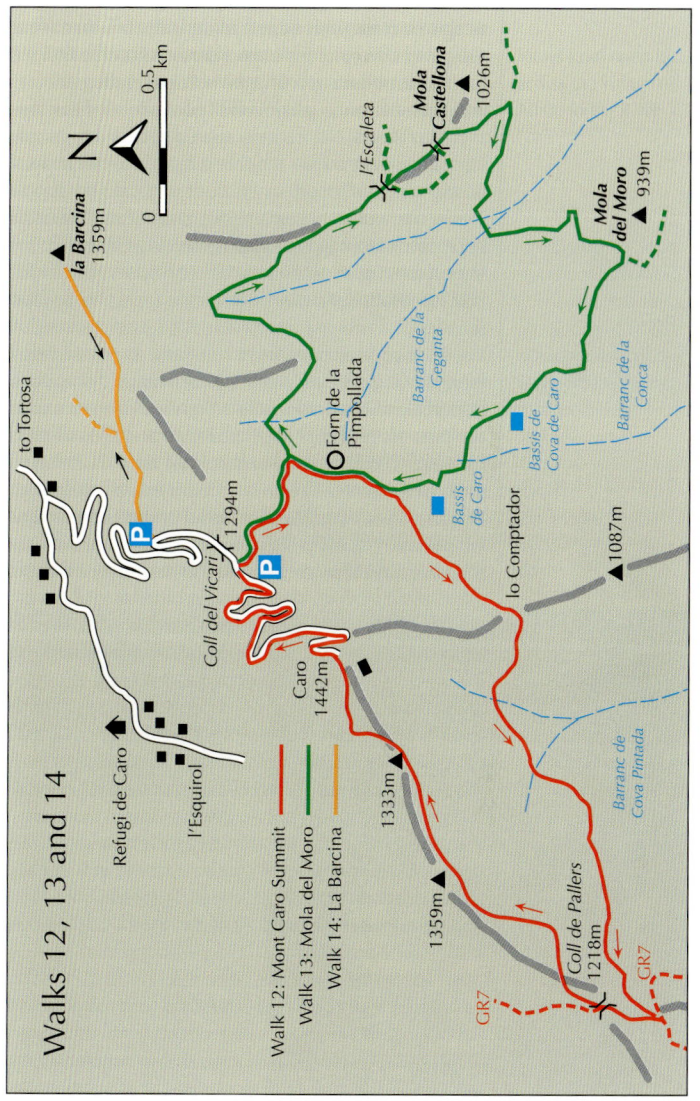

Walks 12, 13 and 14

N

0.5 km

0

to Tortosa

la Barcina 1359m

Refugi de Caro

l'Esquirol

Coll del Vicari 1294m

P

P

Caro 1442m

Forn de la Pimpollada

Barranc de la Ceganta

Bassis de Cova de Caro

Bassis de Caro

lo Comptador

1087m

Mola Castellona 1026m

l'Escaleta

Mola del Moro 939m

Barranc de la Conca

1333m

1359m

Coll de Pallers 1218m

Barranc de Cova Pintada

GR7

GR7

Walk 12: Mont Caro Summit
Walk 13: Mola del Moro
Walk 14: La Barcina

a clear path for 10mins to another signpost. Turn right to continue descending, cross a dry watercourse and rise through woodland. The **Forn de la Pimpollada**, a circular stone-lined hole, is on the left 3mins after crossing the watercourse. Continue over a small rise and, a few minutes later, pass through a gap in a fence to emerge from the woodland. From here the path drops down almost immediately to a junction with a small metal signpost plate. The well-used path to the Bassis de Caro turns left here (return route of Walk 13) but continue straight on, on a clear but substantially smaller path, towards the Coll de Pallers.

Looking back at lo Comptador (the sheep counter)

The path, cairned and waymarked in red, remains overall at approximately the same altitude but undulates constantly to cross the complex terrain. The waymarks are essential and some navigational care is needed. Some 25mins from the start the path passes close beneath an overhanging rock and shortly emerges onto a more open hillside, giving a view of the lo Comptador pinnacles and ridge ahead.

Shortly after, a path joins from the left. Continue straight on, towards a cairn which can be seen directly ahead between the trees. Soon after, the markers lead the route over sloping slabs which are frequently wet. This passage can be avoided by climbing the hillside some 30m further back and traversing above. Some 10mins later the path passes through **lo Comptador** – a dramatic, narrow passage between tall pinnacles. From here the path climbs steeply to cross a subsidiary ridge, and then bears right to contour round a buttress and rise on a balcony route.

Views of the Caro communication station now appear above. The path climbs steeply over rocks at this point before descending through woodland to begin its long traverse of the broad upper reaches of the **Barranc de Cova Pintada**. Some 20mins after rounding the buttress, follow the waymarks to rise over a rocky slab above a dramatic side valley. For the next 35mins the route passes through a jumbled and interesting terrain where care is needed to locate and follow the waymarks. In one place in particular, when the path drops down a grassy slope to cross a dry, pebbly *barranc*, the right turn to climb the opposite slope is not obvious or waymarked. However, cairns and waymarks begin again shortly after the turn.

At about 1hr 50mins from the start the path joins the GR7, at a four-way junction marked with a small metal signpost plate screwed to a rock on the right. Turn right up easy slabs towards the Refugi de Caro following the GR7 (red and white waymarks plus the blue Estels stars) and arrive at the **Coll de Pallers** after 10mins. At the col the GR7 drops to the left, over the ridge, but continue along the ridge, keeping to the left of a large pinnacle following the red waymarks. After a few minutes the path rounds the pinnacle, crosses the ridge and then climbs very steeply on a rocky path towards a large cairn on the skyline. A large black arrow painted on the rock also points the way.

Immediately after the cairn the route passes onto more open, shrubby ground and the telecom masts at the summit of Mont Caro can be seen on the skyline. There are several usable and cairned path lines here; follow those paths which keep close to the top of the ridge and head for a shallow dip on the skyline which, from this position, appears to be about half way between the leftmost cliff and the Caro masts.

The red markers reappear in this dip, culminating in a cairn and a red paint marker on a large rock. This has an arc and a line pointing to the right to indicate a right turn. At this point, 30mins from the Coll de Pallers, the Editorial Piolet maps show the path crossing to the left of the ridge onto very steep ground. This path does not exist on the ground and would be dangerous if it did. Instead, go right at the red paint marker for about 15m, onto higher ground and remain on the right-hand side of the now broad ridge, following a line of cairns leading in the direction of the Caro masts. This leads to a series of three rock bands which are surmounted by some easy scrambling. Cairns and waymarks indicate the best routes.

After the rock bands the ridge narrows and the path passes through a dip before rising and then falling again toward the base of vast, apparently impregnable cliffs reaching up to the Caro summit. At the lowest point, follow the markers across the ridge to the left and enter the woodland by a clear but narrow path. This remarkable path rises safely on the left flank of the cliffs by means of steep wooded ground and sloping terraces, until it can turn upwards to the right in an easy gully. At the top of

Negotiating subsidiary ridges on the eastern side of Mont Caro

this gully it wends its way through more woodland, to emerge by the side of the telecoms station at the summit, some 35mins from the lowest point of the ridge. Join the road and follow it down to the start just before the Coll del Vicari.

Looking back at the pinnacle above the Coll de Pallers

L'ESQUIROL

It is a quite a surprise to come across the little settlement of l'Esquirol, with its houses, hotel, two restaurants and refuge, tucked in behind the summit of Mont Caro. It dates from the beginning of the 20th century, when the more wealthy families of Tortosa started to build summer homes to benefit from the cooler mountain air; frequently renting them to holiday-makers and convalescents with respiratory illnesses. As to the name, the farmer who owned the land on which the little conurbation is built was nicknamed l'Esquirol (the squirrel).

WALK 13

Mola del Moro

Difficulty	Route-finding ●●● Scrambling ●● Exposure ●● (●●● optional)
Total ascent	550m
Time	3hrs 40mins
Distance	8km
Start	Coll del Vicari
Maps	Either Estels del Sud, Editorial Piolet, 1:25,000 (preferred) or El Port Sud, Editorial Piolet, 1:30,000 For route map, see Walk 12.

Note The maps provide general guidance but do not reflect the complex topography or footpath routes of this area accurately. A rope is advised for the optional ascent of the summit of Mola del Moro.

For full directions to start, see Appendix B.

This spectacular circular walk explores the steep and intricate terrain below the summit of Mont Caro. Narrow, airy paths find gaps in cliffs, over ridges, through rock bands and down gorges to circumnavigate the steep ridges which link the Mola Castellona, the Roca del Migdia and the Mola del Moro. There is a 'Lost World' quality to the region, emphasised by the huge cliffs and strangely verdant plateau of the Mola del Moro. The route feels far more strenuous than the 550m of ascent would suggest, partly because of the terrain but mainly because most of the ascent comes in the latter stages. For those with plenty of energy a detour can be made to the summit of Mola Castellona (see Walk 17).

For the most part essential guidance is provided by cairns and waymarks but sustained attention to route finding is needed. There is a short scramble up a chimney at l'Escaleta on the Mola Castellona ridge and a more difficult one onto (and off) the summit of the Mola del Moro. Both are optional.

The start of the walk is approximately 150m beyond the **Coll del Vicari**, at a green signpost marked 'els Bassis de Caro 1hr' and 'la Caramella 3hrs'. Drop down from the road on a clear path for 10mins to another signpost. The sign itself has disappeared but a small metal plate on the post indicates a left turn for la Caramella. For the next 15mins a clear cairned path leads around the head of first branch of the multi-headed Barranc de la Geganta before climbing up into a more rocky landscape. Rounding a buttress opens up airy views of the Montsia and Delta and the path continues to curve around to reveal the broad Ebre valley and Tortosa. Immediately below is the curious cylindrical fortress of the Mola Castellona, circled by tree-covered terraces which surmount its short steep cliffs. Looking to the right the Mola del Moro is also in view, equally fortress-like and separated from the Castellona by the very steep cliffs of the Barranc de la Geganta.

The path continues to curve leftwards to cross a dividing ridge and drop down into the second branch of the **Barranc de la Geganta**. It crosses over to the left bank

Descending from the Coll de Vicari, with the Mola Castellona ahead

some 45mins from the start of the walk and follows the stream course downwards a little way. On reaching an area of stone pillars and pine trees the path makes a short ascent through a rock band to join a ridge above the left side of the *barranc*. Descending along the broad crest of this ridge a cairned grassy col is reached 10mins later. This is **l'Escaleta**, a crossroads of paths marked by a small metal plate on a rock on the ground to the right. To the left is the path for la Caramella by the Raco de la Gralla. At this point there is a choice.

To include the scramble carry straight on, signposted to the Mola Castellona (and la Caramella by a different route), leading directly towards a steep cliff which apparently bars the ridge. Closer inspection will reveal a short chimney by which the top of the cliff can be reached, requiring several rather awkward climbing moves. At the top of the chimney a cairned path leads onward, keeping to the crest of the ridge until a descent to a second, grassy col (unnamed) is made.

To bypass the scramble look for a faint trace of a path bearing right at the l'Escaleta crossroads. This leads across grass and through trees on a faint but cairned path, contouring round the right-hand side of the cliff at its base until the first obvious breach in the cliff can be seen to the left. Climb up to regain the main path at the grassy col.

From the col a clear path rises gently through woodland, bearing to the right side of the **Mola Castellona** summit. It then emerges onto more open grassy slopes. Cairns and red markers guide the descent along one of the Mola Castellona's terraces with the path becoming increasingly stony. About 10 mins from leaving the unnamed col and before the path begins to rise for the ridge ahead, look out for a red painted T-junction waymark and small metal plate, on a rock low down on the left. This indicates an acute right turn, signposted to the Mola del Moro. A cairn and small spot of red paint confirm the location of the path. Although the first few metres look unpromising it does become obvious very quickly. The path meanders up and down, back to the

base of the cliffs just crossed above and then, after 5mins, finds a diagonal ramp to descend more steeply through the cliffs below. Fallen trees tend to obscure this in places but there are regular cairns and red waymarks to confirm the route.

The final rock step onto the summit of the Mola del Moro

Below the ramp the path zigzags down and then bears to the right. The waymarks now become absolutely essential as the path weaves an improbable course above the apparently impregnable cliffs guarding the barranc. Nevertheless, it does find a way to an area of trees and boulders at the bottom of the barranc, where a red marker and cairn indicate a left turn just before the barranc crossing. Cairns then lead onwards to cross the first branch of the barranc some 30mins after leaving the unnamed col.

Very soon the path crosses the second branch of the barranc and, still with cairns and red waymarks, begins to climb towards the next ridge, passing an old limekiln. Some 20mins after crossing the barranc it reaches a small rise from which the col below the Mola del Moro can be seen clearly ahead. The path makes a short, steep

Approaching the Bassis de Cova de Caro

descent at this point to pass the cliffs to the right. There are no immediate red waymarks but the path passes down through a gap with a pillar on the left and then can be seen crossing a narrow ledge below, with a red paint marker on the cliff wall. After this passage it continues more clearly to arrive at the col below the **Mola del Moro** some 12mins later.

There is a crossroads of paths at the col, marked with a red cross and a small metal plate sign. For the optional ascent of the Mola, a path leads off in the direction indicated by the sign. This trends right to pass the first rock barrier and then curves back to arrive at a second barrier, some 8m high. Here, the diagonal break of the ascent line can be seen clearly. The top of the Moro is remarkable: a huge flat area with 360° views, sloping gently up to a large summit cairn. For those without rock-climbing experience a rope to guard the descent from the summit is advisable. In total, the detour takes approximately 20mins and has 30m of ascent.

Leave the col in the direction of the Bassis de Caro. The path, still with red waymarks, climbs steeply towards a pinnacle, around the base of a cliff and then steeply up a gully to the base of the header cliffs, where red markers indicate a left turn, 10mins from the col. Rounding these cliffs the path becomes a balcony route and after 15mins passes above a small water trough, which is the **Bassis de Cova de Caro**. ▶ Soon afterwards the path crosses its final ridge to enter the **Barranc de la Conca** and Mont Caro can now be seen ahead and to the left. Rounding a corner, the path descends slightly through pine trees and overgrown box bushes until, 15mins from the *bassis*, it dives down to the left. Red waymarks confirm the direction but it is not easy to see. About 5mins later there is a crossroads marked with red paint and a small metal plate. Go straight on towards the Bassis de Caro and enter the bed of the dry barranc a minute later, passing a cave on the left.

The path then climbs steeply on the right-hand side of the barranc for 10mins to where the **Bassis de Caro**, a series of hollow tree trunks channelling water from the spring, can be seen to the left. Here another small metal signpost points the way up to the Coll del Vicari and Caro. The objective now is to find the widest and most used of several paths to climb up as directly as possible. After 20mins a T-junction, waymarked in red and with a small metal plate, is reached, pointing right for the Coll del Vicari. Soon the path passes through a broken-down fence with a wooden gate and drops down through trees to pass the **Forn de Pimpollada**, a circular stone-lined hole. At the next junction, some 15mins later, turn acutely left and retrace the outward route to reach the start.

The remains of an animal shelter built into the overhanging cliff to the right show that even this unpromising terrain was used for summer grazing.

WALK 14
La Barcina

Difficulty	Route-finding ● Scrambling ● Exposure ●
Total ascent	80m
Time	1hr 5mins
Distance	3km
Start	Caro Summit Road
Maps	Either Estels del Sud, Editorial Piolet, 1:25,000 (preferred) or El Port Nord, Editorial Piolet, 1:30,000 For route map, see Walk 12.

For full directions to start, see Appendix B.

The short and easy there-and-back walk is on a clear, well-signed path which offers excellent panoramic views from a high mountain situation.

A cool morning on the high Barcina buttress

Follow the signpost marked 'la Barcina' along a rocky path which quickly leads into pinewoods. Where the path forks, after about 10mins, take the right fork to climb gently up to a broad ridge. Old red paint markers confirm the direction and lead up to a dominant rock formation on the ridge. A wooden signpost, marked with a diamond, indicates a small descent to the left. After about 25mins a second wooden post marks a right turn up a small stony gully which leads to a cairn. Just past the cairn is a viewing point with panoramic views down across the river valley and out to sea.

Overlapping ridges seen from la Barcina

Regain the path to continue on up to the summit cairn of **la Barcina**, which is reached about 10mins later. From here the views are spectacular, with the rocky cliffs and deep gorges of the Mola Castellona, la Caramella and the Mola del Moro in the foreground and lines of overlapping ridges reaching along the flanks of the massif to the right. When you are ready, return by the same route.

WALK 15
Cresta del Marturi

Difficulty	Route-finding ●● Scrambling ● Exposure ●●
Total ascent	650m
Time	4hrs 20mins
Distance	12km
Start	Coll de Carrasqueta
Maps	Either Estels del Sud, Editorial Piolet, 1:25,000 (preferred) or El Port Sud, Editorial Piolet, 1:30,000

For full directions to start, see Appendix B.

Starting just beyond the hamlet of l'Esquirol, this circular walk uses the long-distance Estels and GR7 path to climb up through woodland to the Coll de Pallers, or col of the haystacks, so-called because of the two large pinnacles which guard the col. The path follows the line of the Cresta del Marturi, winding below it and traversing the rocky ridges of three remarkable side valleys, affording views of vertiginous descents down to the river plain below. Returning to the other side of the Cresta at one of the few crossing places, the path plunges (dramatically but safely) over the cliffs of the Embarronat escarpment to find its way through deep woodland to the main track back to l'Esquirol.

Take the main track in the direction signposted Cova Avellanes, past the notice about 4x4 vehicles, to reach an alternative parking area 2mins later. From here a path, waymarked in red and white for the GR7 and blue for the Estels, turns left off the main track to climb through woodland, reaching the **Coll de Pallers** after a pleasant climb of 25min or so.

Cross the col, following the sign for the refugi Mas del Frare and the refugi Font Ferrera. The clear path bends to the right and drops steeply along a flat-topped ridge towards a wooded knoll. Although the path (still

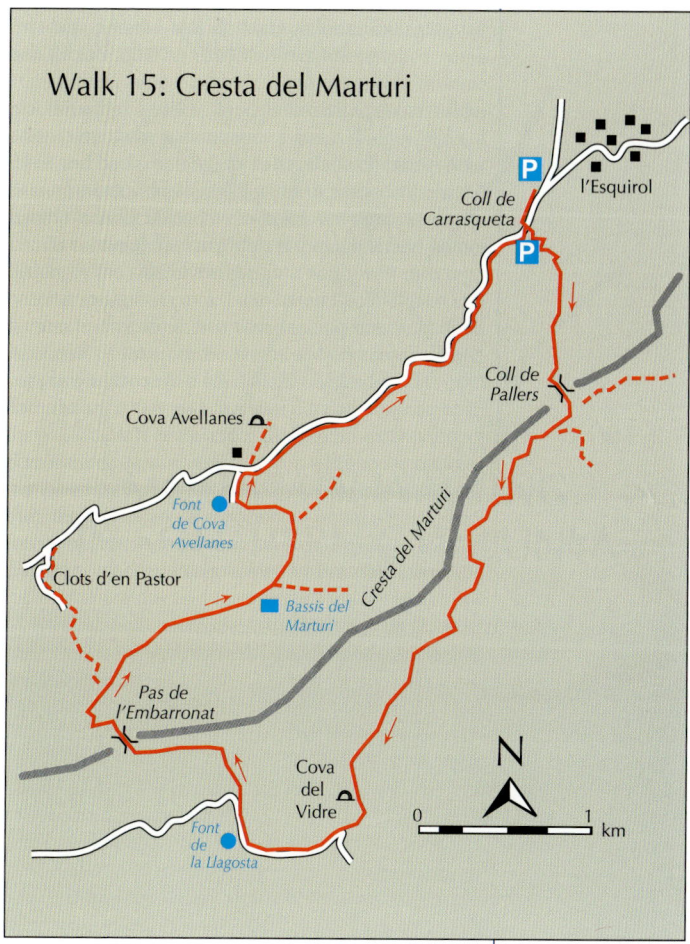

Walk 15: Cresta del Marturi

l'Esquirol

Coll de
Carrasqueta

Coll de
Pallers

Cova Avellanes

Font
de Cova
Avellanes

Clots d'en Pastor

Cresta del Marturi

Bassis del
Marturi

Pas de
l'Embarronat

Cova
del
Vidre

N

Font
de
la Llagosta

0   1
km

waymarked red and white as well as blue) passes to the
left of the little crest, it is also possible to follow the crest
itself and enjoy the spacious panorama opening out on
three sides. Step down to a crossroads of three footpaths
(35min from the start) and turn right.

Looking back along the Cresta del Marturi towards the Coll de Pallers

For 1hr30mins the path weaves and undulates below the Cresta del Marturi, crossing outlying crags, navigating around pinnacles and finding its way over the heads of breathtakingly steep valleys. As it twists and turns, it offers new perspectives ahead of dramatic cross ridges and of the peaks of the Castell d'Airosa and la Joca, before passing by the **Cova del Vidre**. A little further on the path emerges into an open grassy space with a rocky platform on the left. ◄

This is a good place for views of the Barranc de Lloret and the Castell d'Airosa.

Two minutes from the platform the path reaches a broad track. Turn right here in the direction signposted 'Casetes Velles' and 'Refugi Mas del Frare'. Some 9mins along the track, a water reservoir appears on the left and, shortly after, a sign for the **Font de Llagosta**. Approximately 50m after this sign there is a small footpath on the right, marked with a large cairn. This cairned path climbs up a series of terraces for about 10mins, before passing through a gate and continuing up a shallow rocky gully. From here a clear path continues more gently uphill through trees and then crosses an open slope, with good views all around as it reaches a dramatic escarpment. This is the **Pas de l'Embarronat**.

The path turns left along the escarpment, passing a large cairn. Continue for about 5mins, even though the path may seem a little overgrown, and ignore any apparent paths to the (precipitous) right. Just before the true descent path there are some old faded red paint marks on a rock by the left-hand side of the path. The descent path drops to the right immediately after this and is marked with a small cairn and another old red paint mark. From the top, the path looks precipitous but in fact it finds an ingenious and sensible route down some very steep terrain. It is easy to follow and there are also occasional red markers. A junction appears some 12mins after beginning the descent and here a choice can be made.

Continuing on down at this point is the shorter option but the right turn holds more interest, plus an extra 100m or so of ascent. The shorter option goes down via the **Clots d'en Pastor**: follow the clear footpath until it joins a track which, in turn, leads to the main Fredes–Caro track.

The Cova del Vidre

Turn right and follow the track to reach the parking place in approximately one hour.

The main route takes the right turn onto a smaller path, which ascends for 20mins, with occasional red markers until it reaches a terraced clearing. From here the path drops gently down to pass the **Bassis del Marturi** (wooden water trough). Immediately after the Bassis the path divides. Turn left to descend more steeply, following cairns and occasional red markers and pass a large cave, clearly used as an animal shelter. The path now descends for a further 10mins until it reaches a small flat area and then climbs for a few metres. Then the path drops into a slot to the right and descends steeply for 6mins before crossing a loose stony slope. A few more minutes later it reaches a picnic site, some 50mins after leaving the Bassis. This is marked on the map as the **Font de Cova Avellanes** but is signposted as the 'Area Recreativa de Cova Avellanes'. From here a broad path leads on to the main Fredes–Caro track, where the shorter option rejoins the main route. Turn right to return to the parking place in some 35mins' time.

Descending from the Pas de l'Embarronat

WALK 16

Sources of the Matarranya

Difficulty	Route-finding ●● Scrambling ● Exposure ●
Total ascent	530m
Time	3hrs 30mins
Distance	16km
Start	Caro–Fredes track
Maps	Either Estels del Sud, Editorial Piolet, 1:25,000 (preferred) or El Port Sud, Editorial Piolet, 1:30,000

Note The access track is particularly rough and may not be passable in vehicles with particularly low ground clearance.

For full directions to start, see Appendix B.

This circular walk, among the high central valleys and ridges of els Ports, starts with a gentle descent along the Caro–Fredes track, passing through extensive and historic pine forests to reach the head of the Matarranya river gorge. Several *barrancs* converge here to form the source of this important river but the water is mostly underground, leaving a dry gorge of white pebbles framed by water-rounded cliffs. From here the character of the walk changes as the path climbs a steep, wooded barranc past tall cliffs, before emerging on the extensive open pastures of the Clot de Maçana. The return route joins the GR8 path and provides extensive views over the depths and cliffs of the upper reaches of the Ulldemo river valley, before descending to rejoin the Caro–Fredes track.

From the parking place continue along the track, passing the junction with the return path on the right after 15mins – a chain and large white standing stone mark this junction. The recently renovated farmhouses of the Masos de Millers become visible through the trees on the left a few minutes later. After some 1hr 10mins from the

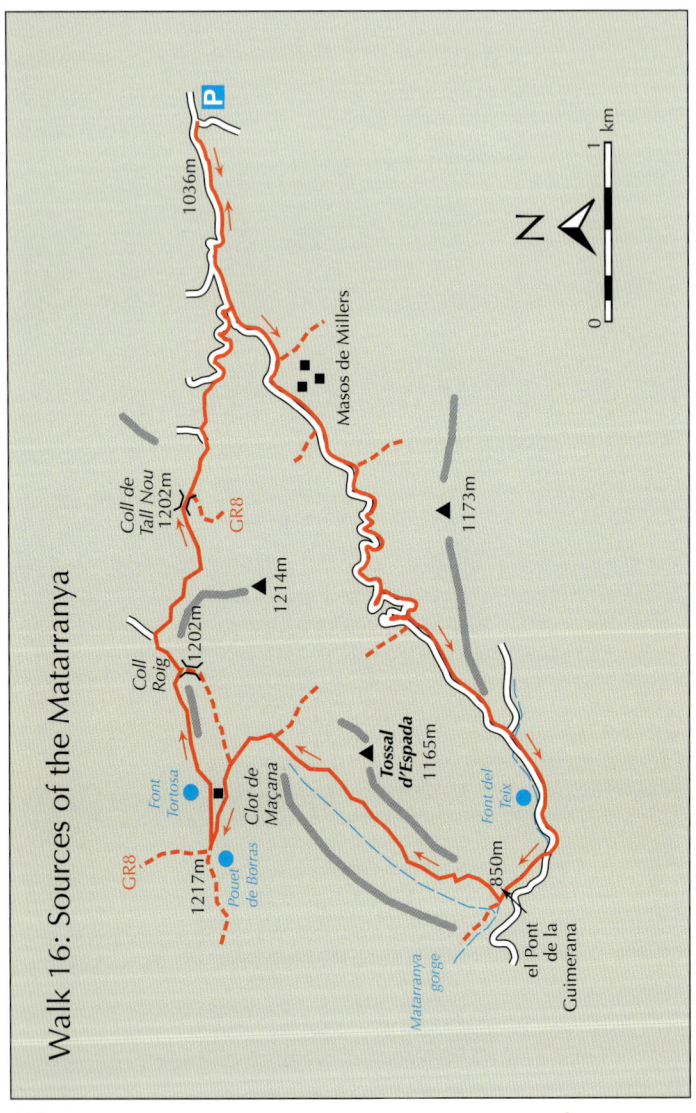

Walk 16: Sources of the Matarranya

Coll de Tall Nou 1202m

GR8

Coll Roig (1202m

1214m

Masos de Millers

1173m

Font Tortosa

Clot de Maçana

Tossal d'Espada 1165m

Font del Teix

1217m

Pouet de Borras

GR8

850m

Matarranya gorge

el Pont de la Guimerana

1036m

P

N

0 — 1 km

start the track enters a picturesque area of rocky outcrops, close to the well-concealed **Font de Teix**. We have yet to encounter anyone who has found this spring!

The track now undulates and then descends more steeply after 10mins to a cairned junction, where a narrower track leads down to the right and the main track climbs steeply to the left. Take the right turn to reach another cairned junction after about 100m. At this point take a narrow path which makes a right turn to descend through bushes for 2mins to reach a flat grassy area. From here the route bears right and follows cairns across the grass. This is the **Pont de la Guimerana**. However, a small path to the left leads down into the head of the (normally) dry **Matarranya gorge**. ▶

It is worth making a short detour here to explore the unusual landscape of the gorge.

From the Pont de la Guimerana a small cairned path leads across a *barranc* and climbs up through tall pines. After 2mins the path divides; take the right fork, which is somewhat obscured by bushes, and continue climbing on a cairned path for a further 15mins to cross a bright orange gully below overhanging cliffs. The valley now starts to narrow and the path remains on its

The head of the Matarranya gorge

105

right-hand side, climbing steeply. Cairns are useful here as the path winds through box bushes to converge with the base of tall undercut cliffs, some 30mins from the start of the ascent. Here a drystone wall has been built to enclose an animal shelter between the cliff and a massive boulder.

As the cliffs curve away to the right, strategically placed cairns indicate the rocky exit from this dramatic place, leading onwards into a flatter area of pine trees and grass. After 15mins the path reaches a T-junction with an overgrown track. Turn left onto the track to bend round to the left and soon it emerges onto the extensive meadows of the **Clot de Maçana** where the path disappears in the grass. A cairn indicates a turn to the left, parallel to an old terrace wall. Further cairns then lead the way up through more terraces, to pass by the ruins of the Mas de Maçana and indicate a stony track climbing away from the meadows. After 10mins the track passes some orange waymarks, tops a ridge and descends quickly to a junction with the red and white waymarked GR8, where a drystone construction covers

The high pastures of the Clot de Maçana

the cistern of the **Pouet de Borras**.

The Pouet (cistern) de Borras

Turn right onto the GR8. This track, narrowing to a path in places, undulates towards the Coll de Tall Nou, offering extensive views out over the upper Ulldemo valley to the left. At a junction, some 5mins from the Pouet de Borras, the route veers right onto a path to pass the **Font Tortosa**. The path then climbs to a junction with another path coming in from the **Coll Roig** to the right, reached after a further 20mins. Ignore a forestry track dropping down to the left soon after and continue for another 15mins to reach the **Coll de Tall Nou**.

At the col the GR8 track bends acutely round to the right to pass a blank concrete signboard. At this point leave the GR8 on a narrow path that carries straight on. Some 14mins after leaving the col the path broadens to become more like a forestry track and loops to the left. Immediately after this bend a cairn and a yellow waymark on a tree indicate a narrow path dropping down to the right. Follow this path (yellow waymarks) for 7mins or so as it descends a band of rock, guided by cairns and yellow waymarks, to reach a forestry track. A right turn along this track leads down to the **Caro–Fredes track** 8mins later. Turn left onto this to return to the start.

LIFE IN ELS PORTS

Even in the high places there are signs of human habitation and land use during the past millennium and earlier. The Moors began to exploit the timber in the ninth century and used local craftsmen to make fine carvings and furniture for prestigious construction projects, such as the Andalus palaces and the Mezquita in Cordoba. Interestingly, there is still ▶

a worldwide furniture industry based around la Senia on the south-west edge of els Ports.

The first use of the high pastures for sheep and goats began in the 12th century and expanded for 700 years as farms were established on the uplands, before declining in the mid-20th century. There is a visible legacy of drystone terrace walls, cisterns, animal troughs, irrigation channels, limekilns, animal enclosures and, above all, farmhouses or *masias*. Self-sufficiency was the key to survival. Extended families shared the *masia* with their animals and grew or foraged everything they needed. Cereals, vegetables, olives, fruit and almonds provided the staples; lime for plaster was quarried locally and fired in the family limekiln and wood was made into furniture, farm implements and kitchen utensils. Firewood was coppiced for heating, cooking and making charcoal. Rushes and palms were woven into baskets, and plants and herbs were gathered and processed for medicines.

Timber continued to be exploited throughout the centuries, especially for shipbuilding – both for wood and for pitch to seal the timbers. Remains of the pitch ovens or *forns de quitra* can still be seen (see walk 12). The ships of the Spanish Armada began life in the forests of els Ports.

(inset) The Mas de Maraco is typical of the isolated farms in use up to the mid-20th century

WALK 17
Roca del Migdia

Difficulty	Route-finding ●●● Scrambling ●●●
	Exposure ●●●
Total ascent	800m
Time	5hrs
Distance	12km
Start	Casa de Carvallo
Maps	Either Estels del Sud, Editorial Piolet, 1:25,000 (covers the upper part of the route only) or El Port Sud, Editorial Piolet, 1:30,000

Note The access track is particularly rough and may not be passable in vehicles with low ground clearance.

For full directions to start, see Appendix B.

Among the more spectacular routes covered in this guide, this one takes in a dramatic and airy ridge, a climb through a small cave, a narrow ledge traverse, a couple of gully scrambles, high grassy terraces of extraordinary beauty and an ingenious descent path amongst tiers of cliffs. The route takes walkers into vertiginous territory normally the preserve of climbers, and there is an option to scale the dramatic summit of Mola Castellona. Roca del Migdia translates as 'mid-day cliff' and is one of a number so-named in els Ports. In previous years these prominent cliffs were used as natural sundials to keep an approximate track of time.

Take the small path which drops down into the *barranc* opposite the old house. Once on the valley floor turn left and then immediately right to climb out of the barranc and rise up leftwards on a small but obvious path. After 2mins the path bends abruptly to the right and then continues zigzagging upwards through prickly vegetation for a further 6mins, when it reaches an apparent junction.

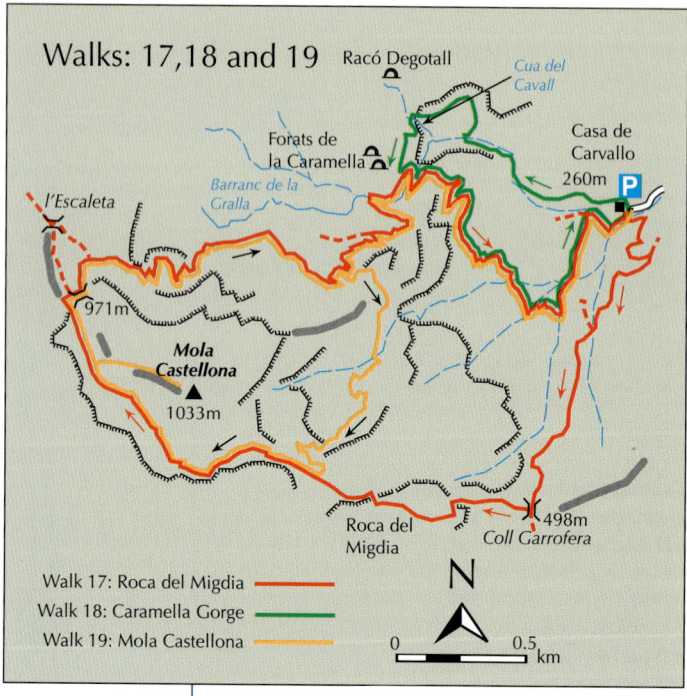

Walks: 17,18 and 19   Racó Degotall

Cua del Cavall

Forats de la Caramella

Barranc de la Gralla

Casa de Carvallo
260m

l'Escaleta

971m

Mola Castellona
▲
1033m

Roca del Migdia   498m
Coll Garrofera

Walk 17: Roca del Migdia
Walk 18: Caramella Gorge
Walk 19: Mola Castellona

N

0   0.5
km

Ignore the small path of red earth which leads off to the right and continue leftwards for a further 2mins to reach another junction, with stones barring the left path. Turn right here and find a red waymark confirming the direction. Some 18mins from the start the path crosses a small side barranc and becomes clearer. Red waymarks guide the way up to reach the obvious **Coll Garrofera** 50mins or so from the start.

Squeeze past a fence to arrive at the junction of two paths on the col. The path to the right begins the climb up the ridge, following cairns and red waymarks. Starting on the left side of the ridge, the path quickly climbs onto its crest and the drama begins. ◄ The path now rounds an outcrop ahead to the left (look out for

Looking down to the right, the Casa de Carvallo can be seen far below over the tops of pinnacles.

strategically-placed red markers) and rejoins the crest with a rocky step up. From here it continues to wind its way up the ridge ingeniously, with the occasional need to use your hands. Some 20mins from the col the path crosses a subsidiary ridge to pass under overhanging cliffs. ▶ A cairn and red marker guide the way to the right, away from the overhanging cliffs and up a rising terrace. At the end of the terrace the route turns left to scramble up a short gully and emerge, 30mins from the col, on a rocky platform with spectacular views of the river, Tortosa, the sea and the Delta.

Impressive caves and arches can be seen down to the right.

The onward route from the platform leaves in an unexpected direction. Follow the cairns left (south-west) to cross to a gap, seen clearly from the rocky platform, between two rocky outcrops and with a tree in the centre. The path rounds a corner 5mins later to reveal a full view of the Roca del Migdia above. This huge cliff of reddish rock seems to present an impossible barrier, but it has a secret. Newly painted red waymarks show the route weaving upward to the extreme right edge of the cliff.

The cave passage through the Roca del Migdia

Approaching the cliff, a red marker on the rock wall itself becomes visible, showing a sharp right-hand turn. In fact, this points up a short rock stairway and into a cave. A short passage (no torch needed) leads out onto a ledge halfway up an enormous cliff. The path follows the ledge to the left on a slightly descending traverse. This passage is not

111

all difficult but looking down on it later leads to feelings of incredulity.

Leaving the ledge, the path is not obvious but there are red markers and cairns which guide, first right and then left, up the main broad gully following on from the direction of the ledge. After a short, easy scramble up a final gully the top of the **Roca del Migdia** is reached, some 45mins from the rocky platform and just over 2hrs from the start of the walk.

At this point there is a junction with the route of **Walk 19**, marked with a red paint sign. A little to the right, a cairn and a metal sign plate also mark the junction. The route of both walks is now upwards to the left and then, shortly after, sharply to the right, following a red marker. A clear cairned path then leads up a grassy slope through pine trees, with the fortress-like cliffs of the Mola Castellona directly ahead. ◄

Cowslips, anemones, miniature daffodils and violets can all be seen here during spring.

Some 15mins from the junction the path reaches a shoulder on the broad grassy terrace below the Mola Castellona. Crossing here opens up new vistas with Mont Caro to the right and the Castell d'Airosa ahead, on one of many overlapping ridges receding into the distance. At this point another path joins from the right, but carry straight on to descend gently past a group of pine trees, growing in limestone pavement and sculpted into bonsai-like forms by the wind. At a junction marked with red paint and a metal plate 5mins later continue straight on and climb diagonally up the hillside on a stony path, towards a stand of pine trees growing in a grassy bank.

Some 5mins after entering the pine trees look out for a large rock on the right with what appears to be a red arrow painted on it and a cairn on top. This marks the starting point for the optional 15min climb up to the summit of the Mola Castellona.

To visit the summit, walk up the grassy slope past the rock, veering right to avoid a rocky outcrop. Turn right along the crest of the broad ridge and continue until the way is barred by another outcrop. A distinct cairned path now appears, leading left around the outcrop. Follow this

along steepish ground until the path climbs right to regain the ridge, 5mins after leaving the main path. Another 5mins later the path veers leftwards to find a short, easy gully which breaches another rock band. The gully slants to the right and emerges into a flat, open space from which the final, small rock step of the ascent can be seen ahead. Look out for 'Moleta Castellona' painted on the rock in orange; this is just next to the best point to climb the step. The **Mola Castellona** summit is flat, grassy and almost circular, with terrific all-round views. Return by the same route.

The main route then continues on for 3mins to reach a well cairned flat and grassy area of the **unnamed col** at 971m. The main path leads on and upwards from here to reach **l'Escaleta**, after which it is possible to turn right onto the main descent path back to the Casa de Carvallo. However, l'Escaleta (ladder) is a somewhat awkward down-climb of a chimney. It is possible to avoid this by using a gully to the right of the unnamed col to converge with the path from l'Escaleta further down.

Looking down at the ledge path and final gully of the Roca del Migdia from the terrace above

113

To do this, look to the right to find a cairn marking a trace of a path leading past box bushes, just before the lowest point of the col. The path quickly disappears, but continue in the same direction for about 30m, where it is possible to descend to the left through a gap in the bushes. There is no obvious path here either, but continue to descend for another 30m to where a path appears leading left. This leads into the bed of the gully, where the descent continues over some small rock steps and through trees until, after about 100m from the col, a very old zigzag path and some cairns appear. These lead shortly into a more open area, sloping down into another shallow gully. Looking ahead and downwards, a trace of a path can be seen on the opposite grassy slope of the gully. Cross over to follow this path to reach a cairned junction with the Escaleta path some 10mins after leaving the unnamed col.

Turn right and continue the descent down the now red waymarked path on steep grass and earth. After a further 10mins the gradient becomes easier and the path finds its way down across the tops of cliffs and down

The Casa de Carvallo in the valley of la Caramella

through easy gullies to reach a T-junction, some 45mins from the unnamed col. Turn left to descend to another junction, some 15mins or so later, and turn right here to continue down for 5mins more to another junction. Turn to the left and drop down into the barranc to cross the stream a couple of minutes later and continue right on the opposite side to a T-junction. Here the route turns right and descends to re-cross the stream but, by continuing straight on, a detour of 5mins can be made to see the **Forats de la Caramella** (caves and rock arches) above the Caramella Gorge.

To continue the descent, return to the last junction and cross the stream, where another T-junction is marked. Turn left here and follow the obvious path, with views back of the Cua del Cavall waterfall, to return to the starting point, reached about 30mins after leaving the Forats de la Caramella.

LA CARAMELLA

The wild and beautiful valleys of la Caramella and la Gralla are poetically named after ancient Catalan wind instruments. Versions of these oboe- and flute-like instruments are still used today to accompany traditional songs and dances. Legend says that the sound of wind and water in these valleys is like the sound of young people singing and dancing.

The small ruined house at the entrance to the Caramella gorge is the Casa de Carvallo, built in 1871 and named after Julio Carvallo Carrion who constructed a system to bring clean water to the city of Tortosa. The system still supplies water for houses lower down the valley.

WALK 18
Caramella gorge

Difficulty	Route-finding ● Scrambling ●●●
	Exposure ●●●
Total ascent	250m
Time	2hrs
Distance	3km
Start	Casa de Carvallo
Maps	El Port Sud, Editorial Piolet, 1:30,000
	For route map, see Walk 17.

Note The access track is particularly rough and may not be passable in vehicles with low ground clearance.

For full directions to start, see Appendix B.

This short but challenging walk contains sections of exposed scrambling in the spectacular Caramella gorge. The route starts quite gently by rising alongside a ladder of pools, often linked by connecting waterfalls. Leaving the pools, there is a very steep climb up the side of the gorge to an airy ledge. This leads on up to the top of a 100m waterfall, the Cua de Cavall, which translates as 'ponytail' in English. At its highest point the route passes the Forats, a series of shallow caves in a steeply undercut cliff.

Leave the car park by climbing the steps at the right-hand side of the **Casa de Carvallo** and then continue up rocks to reach a clear well-made footpath above. Turn left to follow this path as it heads determinedly into a steep-sided and fantastically shaped gorge, to reach the first of a series of small dams and pools after 6mins or so. Here the path leads across a small causeway and up some steps. When the obvious path disappears 2mins later, look for a red arrow on a large rock which indicates a crossing to the opposite bank. The path now rises and scrambles across steep ground above the streambed. After a further 5mins there is a junction where a path drops down right to the river. Continue left to climb and cross an open water conduit before dropping down to the river about 8mins later. The red waymarks lead right to cross the river again, using the dam wall, and the path begins the climb up the steep side of the gorge on the true left bank.

This is a scrambling, zigzagging, meandering and sometimes wet route but it is well waymarked in red. It begins on wet, mossy rock steps and then passes round the left-hand side of a grassy area, before scrambling up leftwards towards the foot of cliffs high above. ▶ After these sections, the route reaches the base of the final cliff where there is a good ledge path traversing to the left above very steep ground. At the end of this traverse the route enters a *barranc*, just above the 100m vertical drop of the **Cua de Cavall** waterfall. Cross the barranc and continue on a rising path, now on the true right bank of the river (approximately 1hr 5mins from the start of the walk). A minute later the path reaches a junction and

On the way there are sections which are steep, rounded and exposed, and which would be difficult to negotiate in reverse because of loose pebbles.

Looking down from near the start of the ascent

The right turn leads to up to a cave, the Racó Degotall, which can be seen above, and is easily reached.

a small cave. Turn left to make the final scramble of the route up good rock, following worn red markers, to reach a cairn and a very good path. ◄

The left turn continues the route to reach a spectacular viewing platform, from which the whole of the scrambling ascent can be seen. After this, the red waymarked path continues to the **Forats de la Caramella**, a series of shallow caves in undercut cliffs. After passing the forats a T-junction is reached in 3mins. Clear marking in red paint indicates Mont Caro ahead and the forats behind. Turn left here to drop down into the barranc and cross a stream. On the other side of the stream turn left at another T-junction to follow the obvious path (cairns and red markers). As this rocky path rises alongside the gorge there are further opportunities for superb views of the Cua de Cavall and of the ascent route in relation to it. The path then crosses a subsidiary ridge and begins the descent back all the way to the starting point at Casa de Carvallo.

A series of rock pools are encountered in the gorge

WALK 19
Mola Castellona

Difficulty	Route-finding ●● Scrambling ●● Exposure ●●
Total ascent	800m
Time	4hrs 15mins
Distance	10km
Start	Casa de Carvallo
Maps	Either Estels del Sud, Editorial Piolet, 1:25,000 (covers the upper part of the route only) or El Port Sud, Editorial Piolet, 1:30,000 For route map, see Walk 17.

Note The access track is particularly rough and may not be passable in vehicles with low ground clearance.

For full directions to start, see Appendix B.

Arriving at the Casa de Carvallo it is immediately obvious that the terrain of la Caramella is steep, dramatic and difficult. But this is a circular route that manages to reach the summit of the fortress-like Mola Castellona without difficult scrambling or vertiginous exposure. It is of course strenuous: climbing more or less relentlessly up for 800m and then descending just as directly. Yet there is nothing predictable or obvious about the route, as it climbs up gullies, around cliffs, over ridges and onto viewpoints. The paths are clear and well waymarked, which is fortunate since they, and the terrain, are too convoluted to be well represented on the Editorial Piolet maps.

Take the path past the **Casa de Carvallo** and then branch right at the junction immediately after. Shortly after, following red waymarks, the path drops down into the *barranc*, to cross and continue on the opposite side. After a minute or so there is a second junction at which the route takes the left path, indicated again by a red waymark. A

119

minute later, at the next junction, there is another left turn, to move away from the line of the main barranc. The route now stays with this path to climb a side barranc, cross some water-worn rock and pass a ruined building. After a further 5mins the path makes a right-angle turn to the right and starts to make its way clearly and determinedly up the hillside – still with red waymarks.

Half an hour into the walk, the path turns unexpectedly to the right among bushes. Look out for a rock on the right of the path with a red marker and a cairn on top and the right turn is just a metre or two further on. Continuing straight on at this point would lead to a steep gully. Some 10mins after the turn the path climbs a rocky slope to reach a ridge, where a red T-junction marker indicates a right turn for a short detour out to a viewpoint. The route continues straight on to cross the ridge and descend slightly, with views of the spectacular Cua de Cavall (ponytail) waterfall and the depths the Caramella gorge below.

The cliffs and terraces below the Mola Castellona recede to form a cirque

The path now arrives quickly at a T-junction, marked by red paint. Turn right here to cross the **Barranc de la Gralla**

The improbable summit of the Mola Castellona

and zigzag right and then left on its opposite side to reach another red-painted T-junction a few minutes later. Turning left here, on the path signposted to Caro, continue alongside the stream for a minute or so before crossing back by means of a stepping stone. A red waymark can be seen on a rock on the opposite side and the crossing is some 50mins from the start of the walk.

The path now goes leftwards and climbs for 2mins to reach a junction marked with a red paint spot. Turn right and 5mins later reach another junction, marked by a cairn and a red mark. Taking the left turn, a steep diagonal up the hillside leads, after 10mins, to a short section of gully with a small cave to the right. After this, continuing upwards for a further 5mins leads to a junction marked by a cairn. The clear path to the right is the return route. Take the left branch, even though the way soon becomes obscured by bushes. Once through them a red marker on a rock confirms the way and the path becomes more obvious. After a little while the path levels out briefly and opens out to give good views. But, it very soon resumes its ascent to climb over a shoulder

121

and turn a (large) corner of the cliffs into a very different landscape, entering a cirque topped by high cliff walls.

The gradient relents as the path passes through bushes and into unexpectedly pastoral terrain before resuming its ascent. Still clearly cairned and waymarked in red, it climbs obliquely up a rock band and on to a steep rocky path; finding a way to breach the cliffs above and exit the cirque. Approximately 30mins from the last junction, it gains the foot of some undercut cliffs and then some 4mins later emerges onto the grassy terraced top of the cirque, where a red marker indicates a right-angle turn to the left. The path now descends slightly to make its way along the top of a huge buttress. After 3mins or so a cairn marks a junction and just below it there is a small metal signpost plate fastened to a rock. There is also a paint marker, a little closer to the cliff edge. At this point the route turns right to join that of **Walk 17**, and the remainder of the circuit is described there. Before leaving, it is worth glancing to the left over the chasm to see the improbable trace of the ledge path used in Walk 17 to reach the junction.

WALK 20

Lloret high level route

Difficulty	Route-finding ●● Scrambling ●●
	Exposure ●●
Total ascent	1000m
Time	6hrs
Distance	17km
Start	At the end of the Barranc de Lloret road
Maps	Either Estels del Sud, Editorial Piolet, 1:25,000 (preferred) or El Port Sud, Editorial Piolet, 1:30,000

For full directions to start, see Appendix B.

This long and strenuous excursion is a good way to experience the cliffs and pinnacles of the magnificent Barranc de Lloret and its tributaries. Steepness is the key word but the paths manage to negotiate the territory without vertiginous exposure. Fixed wooden ladders (*escarrisó*) provide an easy exit from the narrow Borosa cleft to provide access to the Coll dels Morralets. At the col there is an alternative lower-level tour of the Lloret, marked on the map and waymarked on the ground. This is an option only for longer days and for those who like awe-inspiring scrambling and exposure combined with prickly undergrowth and difficult paths. Above the col a good path climbs through a wild and beautiful landscape to join the long-distance GR7 path. This traverses above the savage and almost inaccessible *barrancs* d'Orio and Baretes before descending to return on easy tracks.

Take the right fork at the car parking space to follow by the side of the (sometimes dry) river. After 5mins or so the track narrows to a path and then crosses the river on a wooden bridge. At the other side turn left and follow the river on its true left bank. After approximately 6mins the path passes a sign indicating the *bufadors* or resurgences down to the left and a minute later the path divides. The route turns right here, to follow red markers and begin

123

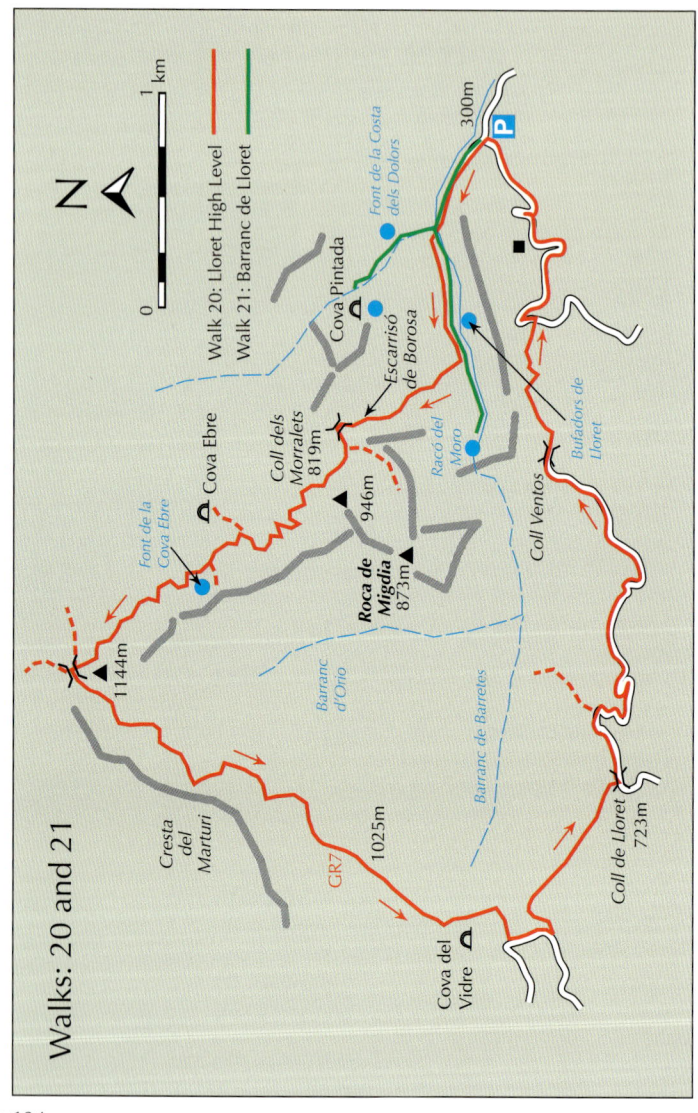

Walks: 20 and 21

N

0 — 1 km

Walk 20: Lloret High Level
Walk 21: Barranc de Lloret

300m

Font de la Costa
dels Dolors

Cova Pintada

Escarrisó
de Borosa

Cova Ebre

Coll dels
Morralets
819m

Font de la
Cova Ebre

946m

Racó del
Moro

Bufadors de
Lloret

Roca de
Migdia
873m

Coll Ventos

1144m

Barranc
d'Orio

Barranc de Barretes

Cresta
del
Marturi

1025m

GR7

Coll de Lloret
723m

Cova del
Vidre

the climb away from the river and up towards the pinnacles above. After a further 5mins there is another junction where a small metal signpost plate indicates that the route turns right again for the Escarrisó de Borosa. The path now climbs to pass to the right of some shallow caves and a cairn shows the way. Some 15mins later the cairned path twists and turns to avoid gully scrambles, although the red waymarks suggest tackling them (optional).

The climb continues for half an hour to reach an unexpected patch of scree with a fig tree growing in the middle of it. After ascending the scree the path turns left to climb towards the base of some undercut cliffs. The way now becomes increasingly hemmed in by cliffs and pinnacles until it narrows to a cleft, with two wooden ladders leading up over the top providing the only exit. This is the **Escarrisó de Borosa** and it is reached some 1hr 20mins from the start of the walk. A further 10mins of climbing on a clear path leads on to a grassy plateau and up to the shapely rock pillars of the **Coll dels Morralets**. Turn left here for Cova Ebre and Pallers following a red painted arrow on the back of the first pillar. About 10m further

Looking back over the route from above the scree with the fig tree

Pinnacles at the Coll dels Morralets

on there is a rock on the right-hand side of the path with a metal signpost plate. The route carries straight on here, through woodland, towards the Cova Ebre and Caro.

The path, cairned and waymarked in red, now zig-zags up steeply to emerge from the trees after about 10mins and climb a grassy hillside. It re-enters woodland after 20mins and reaches a T-junction, marked as such in red paint. Turn left and, less than a minute later, find another junction marked with a cairn. The left path is for the Font de la Cova Ebre but the route bears right to curve around a large boulder and then pass a tiny metal sign-post embedded in a rock a metre or so to the right. Stay with the obvious path, climbing slightly and following the direction for the Coll de Pallers. It now leads across an area of dead trees and on towards a large, chunky rock pillar on the ridge ahead. Occasional worn red mark-ers and cairns confirm the way as the path negotiates some complicated terrain and then climbs up to cross a ridge, near the spot height for 1144m on the map. It then descends to a substantial path crossroads – reached approximately 1hr 5mins from the Coll dels Morralets.

The crossroads is copiously marked, with a metal signpost cross, red and white waymarks for the GR7 long-distance footpath and blue stars for the Estels route. Turn left here for the Cova del Vidre, following both sets of waymarks. The path descends and then traverses, weaving and undulating below the cliffs of the **Cresta del Marturi** to navigate across outlying crags and around pinnacles. As it twists and turns, it offers new perspectives ahead of dramatic cross ridges and of the peaks of the Castell d'Airosa and la Joca, but most of all it allows glimpses of the wild and inaccessible scenery of the Barrancs d'Orio and Baretes down to the left. After 1hr 30mins the **Cova del Vidre** is reached; a minute or so later turn left onto open pastures with a limestone pavement platform guarding the cliff edge. ▶

The route continues across grass towards a substantial track; turn left here following directions for la Galera and Casa Forestal. Some 4mins later look out for a path dropping down acutely to the left, marked with a cairn. This path is waymarked with occasional red markers; it is rough and rocky and occasionally overgrown. After 20mins it enters and descends a shallow rocky gully alongside an overhanging cliff. After leaving the gully the path, still waymarked in red, makes its way onto the top of a ridge and continues down for 10mins more to reach a vague T-junction. A left turn leads to the **Coll de Lloret** track some 10mins later.

Turn left onto the track to follow its winding route back along the length of the Barranc de Lloret. ▶ After half an hour the track comes to an end at the **Coll Ventos**. Here the route passes through a stile to continue descending more steeply on a red waymarked footpath, coming to a makeshift gate after about 20mins and heading for the track that can be seen ahead. Turn left on the track to descend gently and reach some enclosures where bulls can usually be seen grazing. Continue on the track above these and pass through a wide metal gate onto a semi-paved road. Turn right here to descend to some locked gates just above the parking. A pedestrian gate at the right gives access to the start, approximately 1hr 15mins from the Coll de Lloret.

From this excellent viewpoint the return track can be seen far below over the wild ridges and pinnnacles of the Barranc d'Orio.

On the left there are spectacular views of the cliffs, crossed earlier in the walk.

WALK 21
Barranc de Lloret

Difficulty	Route-finding ● Scrambling ● Exposure ●
Total ascent	70m to the Cova Pintada; 80m to the Racó del Moro
Time	50mins there and back to the Cova Pintada, 1hr there and back to the Racó del Moro
Distance	4km
Start	At the end of the Barranc de Lloret road
Maps	Either Estels del Sud, Editorial Piolet, 1:25,000 (preferred) or El Port Sud, Editorial Piolet, 1:30,000 For route map, see Walk 20.

For full directions to start, see Appendix B.

This easy walk comprises two separate there-and-back excursions within one of the els Ports most beautiful valleys (for more information on els Ports' see Walk 16). The Barranc de Lloret runs almost parallel to the main els Ports ridge and climbs steeply to cross one of its dramatic subsidiary ridges at the Coll de Lloret. Deeply-scored side *barrancs* rise up from the valley floor, dissecting towering cliffs to reach the main ridge. The short routes described here stay within the lower valley, to explore some of its interesting geological features.

Take the right fork at the car parking space to follow an unsurfaced track by the side of the (often dry) river. After 5mins or so the track narrows to a path and then crosses the river on a wooden bridge. At the other side there is a junction: the path to the right climbs up a side valley to the Cova Pintada, while the left path stays in the main valley and leads to the Racó del Moro.

Take the right path and climb up the side of the ever-steepening side valley towards the rock wall ahead.

The path remains obvious and easy to follow all the way and reaches the large, undercut rockwall of the **Cova Pintada** some 30mins from the start of the walk.

Return to the wooden bridge by the same route (20mins) and this time take the left turn to follow the true left bank of the river. After about 6mins there is a small wooden signpost on the left indicating the path to the Bufadors de Lloret. The narrow path leads down to the riverbed where, after wet weather, water bubbles up from a series of resurgences.

Returning to the main path, the walk continues for a minute to a junction of paths. Take the left path which drops into the floor of the *barranc* and then disappears, leaving you to weave a way up the dry riverbed towards the foot of the final cliffs. It is not in any way difficult to negotiate a route up through this final section of the walk but it does require squeezing past blocks, hopping on boulders and, in the final stages, edging around rock pools. The **Racó del Moro** (The Moor's corner) is reached some 30mins from the wooden bridge but when the waterfall is not running there is nothing to mark the place. On the other hand, the impressive ring of cliffs here makes it obvious that the route goes no further without rock-climbing gear. Return to the wooden bridge (30mins) by retracing the same route, taking care to locate the path which exits the barranc to the left and which is marked with red waymarks.

Looking towards the cliffs guarding the Cova Pintada

WALK 22
Roca Xapada

Difficulty	Route-finding ● Scrambling ● Exposure ●●
Total ascent	550m
Time	2hrs 15mins
Distance	6km
Start	By the wooden bridge at the entrance to the Racó d'en Marc
Maps	Either Estels del Sud, Editorial Piolet, 1:25,000 (preferred) or El Port Sud, Editorial Piolet, 1:30,000

For full directions to start, see Appendix B.

The geological formations of the Racó d'en Marc and the Racó dels Capellans are extraordinary. Ranks of rock pinnacles, like organ pipes sculpted by Salvador Dali, tower over the walker. The path winds among them and then climbs above them, to emerge high on a rocky ridge dominated by the Castell de l'Airosa. Here there are dramatic views of tiered cliffs dropping down to the Lloret valley and vistas of rocky ridges in all directions. The walk visits the col below the Castell and then continues up to the rocky terraces below the Roca Xapada before returning by the same route.

Cross the footbridge and follow the sign indicating the Racó de la Cova d'en Marc and l'Airosa. The obvious path leads up a rocky ravine to reach the **Cova d'en Marc** in about 5mins. Climb up into the entrance to find a path that continues to the right and climbs up to the left of a pillar. About 5mins later turn left at a junction, signposted to l'Airosa, and continue climbing on a very clear and well-made path up to the head of the ravine. After 15mins or so the path crosses a mostly dry river bed. A further signpost for l'Airosa shows the way onward. The route continues climbing through an extraordinary landscape until it reaches a junction just below the ridge, some

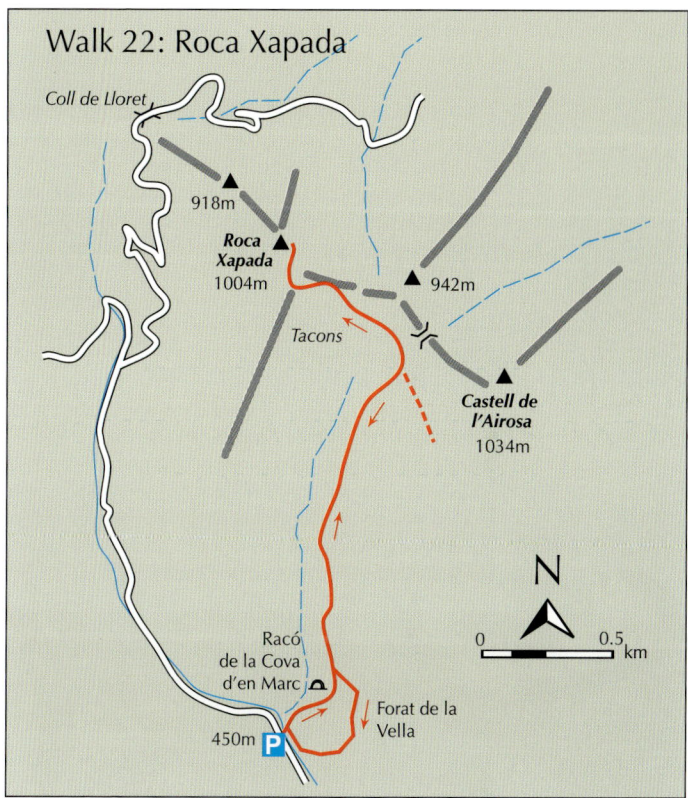

Walk 22: Roca Xapada

Coll de Lloret

918m

Roca Xapada
1004m

942m

Tacons

Castell de l'Airosa
1034m

Racó de la Cova d'en Marc

Forat de la Vella

450m 🅿

N

0   0.5
          km

50mins from the start. Where a signpost indicates a right turn for l'Airosa, turn left on to an unsigned and less well-made path that heads away from the Castell de l'Airosa towards some jagged rock formations on the ridge.

Follow the occasional red markers and cairns below these rocks, on a rising traverse which, after 18mins or so, joins the ridge at some airy gaps. ▶ Looking away from the drop, there are vistas of majestic ridges all around and the sea is visible glinting out to the horizon on the left. The now rather indistinct path continues climbing for

Looking over to the right the vertical cliffs drop away to the Lloret valley.

131

a further 5mins to reach a col with a cairn and a rock pillar guarding each side. Cross the col and follow the red markers downwards on a clever path which finds its way along a narrowing ridge. After a few minutes the path emerges from the undergrowth at the foot of the cliffs of the **Roca Xapada**. Those with a good head for heights can use the broad flat rocks here as a viewpoint. The path does however continue on down a little way to a larger, less airy stony platform from which to admire the views. It is worth noting that the red markers do indicate an onward path leading down to the Coll de Lloret but this is not advised since the route is steep and complicated and the markers are misleading.

The return is by the same route until a signposted junction is reached above the **Cova d'en Marc**. Take the left path, signposted to the **Forat de la Vella** and the Barranc de la Vall, for an unmissable treat. The path descends on made steps to pass through the Forat de la Vella, a wonderful natural arch, before continuing to the valley floor and turning right along an irrigation channel to regain the wooden bridge 55mins from the Roca Xapada.

Looking back through the Forat de la Vella

WALK 23

Font del Paradis

Difficulty	Route-finding ● Scrambling ● Exposure ●
Total ascent	540m
Time	3hrs 20mins
Distance	10km
Start	Area de lleure de la Vall (la Vall picnic site)
Maps	Either Estels del Sud, Editorial Piolet, 1:25,000 (preferred) or El Port Sud, Editorial Piolet, 1:30,000

For full directions to start, see Appendix B.

The easy circular walk provides changing perspectives of the towering cliffs of the Faixes Tancades topped by the improbable peaks of la Joca and the Mola dels Conills. The clearly marked path ascends through woodland before crossing a stream at the head of the broad barranc of la Vall and returning to the picnic site on good tracks and paths. The route has been equipped with marker posts and signposts and is waymarked throughout in red.

Take the broad track leading on from the picnic site, passing the signpost indicating the Mas de Barró and the Font del Paradis. After 100m or so the track crosses the stream and continues on to an open grassy space. A small path leads to the left out of this clearing, signposted 'Font del Paradis'. Follow this path to climb up into the woodland. Gaps in the trees allow glimpses of the curious la Joca peak. At a junction some 15mins from the start, with red markers in both directions, continue straight on as indicated by a small post with a red diamond marker. The path now passes below the tall Faixes Tancades cliffs to reach another signpost indicating the route to the Font del Paradis. At the next junction, some 15mins later, the

Walks 23 and 24

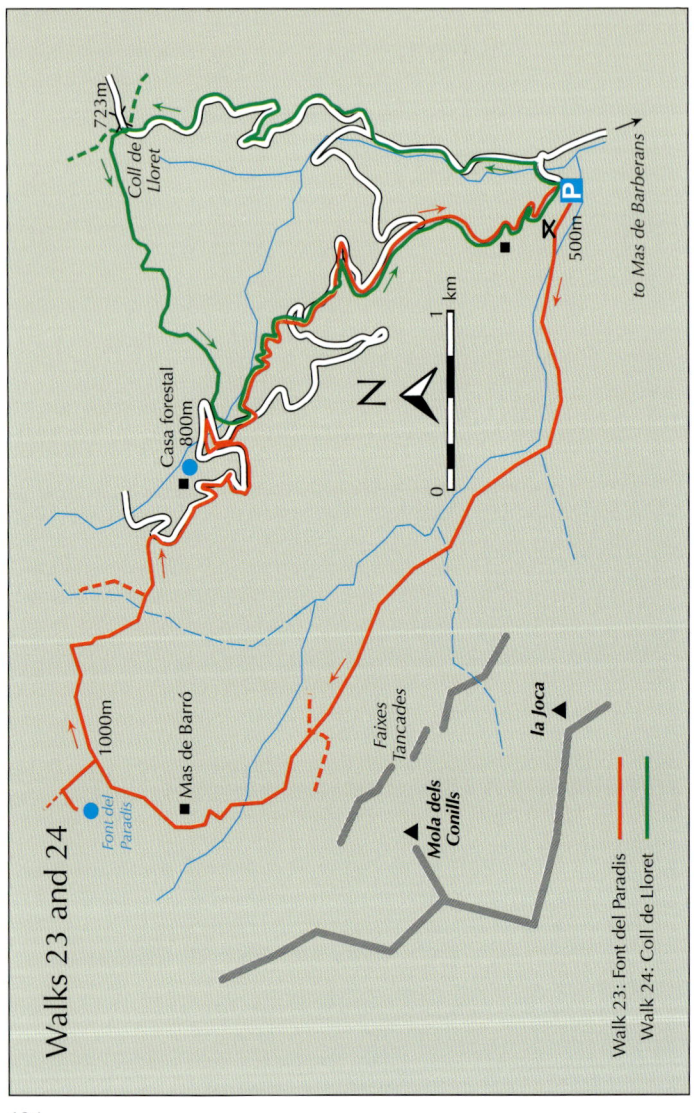

723m

Coll de Lloret

to Mas de Barberans

P

500m

1 km

N

Casa forestal 800m

1000m

Font del Paradis

Mas de Barró

Faixes Tancades

la Joca

Mola dels Conills

Walk 23: Font del Paradis

Walk 24: Coll de Lloret

red markers indicate a left turn but the route continues straight on in the direction indicated by another post with the red diamond marker.

The path now climbs and crosses a *barranc*, often with running water, and reaches the ruined **Mas de Barró**, just over an hour from the start. Continue to the left, following the sign for the Font del Paradis and the Casa Forestal to climb more steeply for 10mins and reach a viewing point. Look out for some rocks to the right of the path and a small footpath leading onto them. Here the full extent of the Faixes Tancades, overtopped by the Mola dels Conills, can be seen to the right, while to the front the valley reaches down, overlooked by the dramatic forms of the Castell de l'Airosa and Roca Xapada (see map for Walk 22).

Some 10mins later the path crosses a wet area and joins another footpath. A signpost points left for the Font del Paradis 450m. To visit the Font, follow the path upwards for 5mins to another signpost indicating a left turn for the font. Contouring for 3mins the path now enters a muddy area where some log-supported steps lead quickly down to the **Font del Paradis**. ▶ Return by the same path to the junction with the Font del Paradis 450m signpost.

It is clearly a paradise for wild boar since evidence of their rootings and wallowings can be seen all around.

The route now goes straight on, descending towards the Casa Forestal on an ancient animal pasturing path. At a T-junction, 15mins later, a cairn indicates a right turn along a path which leads down to the main La Valls forestry track. Turn right along the track which leads down to the **Casa Forestal**, or follow the shortcuts which cut off the bends in the track and which are clearly marked by posts with red diamonds.

The remainder of the descent is really a matter of personal preference. The track continues down to the picnic site in a series of loops and the path with its posts and red diamonds takes a more direct line, crossing and re-crossing the track, so the routes can be mixed and matched according to whim. The path is not well made in the early parts of the descent so the track may be prefereable here, but the path is preferable for the lower

The Font del Paradis stretches as it passes some picturesque ruined buildings. The path emerges directly onto the picnic site, but if you come down the track look out for the acute right turn onto the track that crosses the main Galera barranc and leads to the picnic site and car park. The la Vall picnic site is reached in approximately 1hr 45mins from the Font del Paradis.

WALK 24
Coll de Lloret

Difficulty	Route-finding ● Scrambling ● Exposure ●
Total ascent	300m
Time	1hr 45mins
Distance	6km
Start	Area de lleure de la Vall (la Vall picnic site)
Maps	Either Estels del Sud, Editorial Piolet, 1:25,000 (preferred) or El Port Sud, Editorial Piolet, 1:30,000 For route map, see Walk 23.

For full directions to start, see Appendix B.

This pleasant and easy circular walk follows good tracks and paths that lead up to the Coll de Lloret, dramatically overlooked by the Roca Xapada. The route then contours on sheltered, south-facing slopes at the head of the Barranc de la Galera before descending through woodland back to the picnic site.

Walk back from the picnic site to rejoin the main valley track and turn left. The track climbs gently for 12mins or so to a junction where a smaller track, sometimes with a chain across, leads to the right. Take this track to climb up steadily. As it rounds the last bends before the col, the line of the onward path becomes visible across the hillside. The **Coll de Lloret** is reached some 35mins from the start and from here the route continues on a small footpath, marked with a red waymark and a cairn, climbing up to the left. However, it is worth making a short detour along the track to look down into the beautiful Lloret valley.

Return to the col and take the small footpath, which almost immediately branches and the route takes the left

Leaving the Coll de Lloret to contour around south-facing slopes, with la Joca in the background

branch. The clear narrow path now contours around sheltered south-facing hillsides. There are fine views ahead of the singular peak of la Joca flanked by the steep cliffs of the Faixes Tancades. About 20mins from the col the path drops to continue under water-sculpted cliffs and then climbs to join a broad track some 15mins later.

Turn left onto this track, which leads back down to the picnic site in a series of big loops. There is a good path which criss-crosses the track to shortcut the loops and the first section of it is to be found approximately 100m along the track, on the left. Look for the wooden post with a red diamond on it (see end of Walk 23). All the shortcuts are signposted in this way and so are easy to find and follow back to the la Vall picnic site which is reached in approximately 1hr 10mins from the col.

WALK 25

Sant Roc to Arnes and back

Difficulty	*Day 1, main route*: Route-finding ●● Scrambling ●● Exposure ● *Day 1, variant*: Route-finding ● Scrambling ● Exposure ● *Day 2*: Route-finding ●● Scrambling ● Exposure ●
Total ascent	*Day 1, main route*: 700m; *variant*: 650m; *Day 2*: 750m
Time	*Day 1, main route*: 5hrs 45mins; *variant*: 5hrs 20mins; *Day 2*: 6hrs 15mins
Distance	*Day 1, main route*: 22km; *variant*: 26km; *Day 2*: 25km
Start	Ermita Sant Roc
Maps	Either Estels del Sud, Editorial Piolet, 1:25,000 (preferred) or El Port Nord, Editorial Piolet, 1:30,000

For full directions to start, see Appendix B.

This is a long two-day circular walk that explores fully the multi-faceted nature of els Ports. The crossing covers an unparalleled variety of landscape, geology, atmosphere and walking terrain with opportunities for encountering ibex, red squirrels, eagles, choughs and many woodland birds. The colonies of nesting griffon vultures on the high, inaccessible ledges of the spectacular Roques Benet can easily be seen. The western side of els Ports is characterised by rounded, sculptural rock formations and steep-sided river gorges (estrets), and in some there is water flowing all year round. After heavy rain the river gorges can remain full enough to obstruct walkers for a week or more. The main route for Day 1 is the more adventurous, involving some boulder-hopping and easy scrambling in the beds of two *barrancs*. If there is too much water in the first barranc, a back-track of 25mins allows ▶

Walk 25: St Roc to Arnes

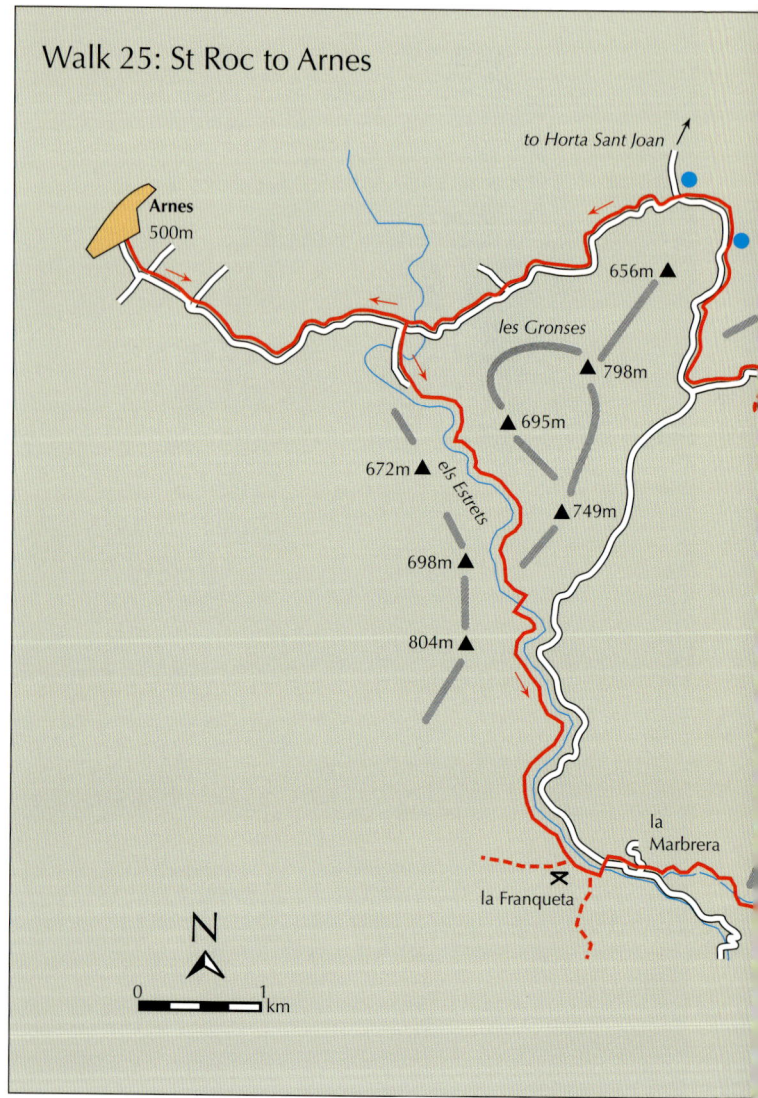

to Horta Sant Joan

Arnes
500m

656m ▲

les Gronses

▲ 798m

▲ 695m

672m ▲ els Estrets

▲ 749m

698m ▲

804m ▲

la Marbrera

la Franqueta

N

0 1 km

Estret del Boter

Mas de Fandos

▲787m

▲776m

▲1078m

Sant Roc
450m
P

931m   ▲

1076m   ▲

Font Canaleta

Coll de les Canals

Font de Carrasca

968m   ▲

▲1016m

Roques Benet

Mas de les Eres

▲1073m

Coll de Membrado

1121m   ▲

1117m   ▲

1028m   ▲

Coll de l'Enrelojada

▲1146

Coll d'Alfara

1204m   ▲

1203m   ▲

1084m   ▲   ■ Mas de Maraco

▲983m

1068m   ▲

1085m   ▲

Carrer Ample

a return to complete the route by the variant, avoiding the potentially wet passages and all scrambling. There is also a dry route option for the second barranc, with a 30min back-track.

Day 1

From Sant Roc follow the circuit route for **Walk 3** over the **Coll de les Canals** and the Coll del Bassot until the path joins a wide well-made track as it loops at the bottom of the valley, approximately 1hr 35mins from the start. Here the main and variant routes for Day 1 diverge.

Main route

Turn right to continue parallel to the course of the stream in the valley bottom and pass the Font de Carrasca, a series of stone drinking troughs. Continue on the track as it loops to cross the stream, and pass the path on the right up to the **Font Canaleta**, 20m or so up the path. After a minute the grassy track re-crosses the stream and, after a further 4mins or so, bends to the left to climb away from the stream. Here a cairn marks a small path dropping down to the right. This path continues close to the stream, crossing and recrossing until, some 12mins or so after leaving the track, it enters the stream bed proper. ◄ At this point it will become clear if the way ahead is passable. If not, return past the two fonts to the junction where the routes diverge (approximately 25mins) and continue by the variant route.

Steep rock slopes on either side constrain the route.

If the route is passable, continue in the bed of the *barranc* for a 5min passage through a narrow gorge. When the cliffs open out, look to the left for a cairn which marks a small path leading along the true left bank of the stream bed. This cairned path crosses and recrosses the stream bed, to emerge into an area of fields and terrace walls which leads on to the ruins of an extensive old farm, the **Mas de Fandos**. Pass the first building and climb up to pass the right-hand side of a second, where the path joins the blue waymarked Estels route. Turning left, a wooden signpost marks the start of the dry route option. It states, *Ruta alternativa en cas de crescuda del barranc.* It might be necessary to return to this point if the second barranc should prove to be impassable.

Take the Estels route down into the barranc, following both blue and yellow and white waymarks. After 20mins or so the paths diverge at a small signpost and the route turns sharply left for Arnes, descending and following blue Estels waymarks and occasional red markers. The path now enters the **Estret del Boter**, a narrow gorge. This requires some easy scrambling for 10mins to pass along it and then to exit with the help of a chained section. Emerging from the gorge, the path continues steeply up through trees for 8mins or so to join the dry route option path at a signpost.

The blue-waymarked path now continues straight on for Arnes, topping a rise and then descending to a ruined building some 10mins later. After crossing a stream, the path begins its final climb (approx 150m) with the imposing **Roques Benet** looming ever larger. After 15mins the path joins a track and then almost immediately leaves it to follow a blue waymarked path to the right. The path rejoins the track after a further 5mins. Turn right here to descend to a junction with a broader track. This is where the variant

Leaving the Estret del Boter

route rejoins, some 2hrs 30mins after diverging. Turn right to reach a paved road some 15mins later, where a signpost indicates multiple walking and cycling routes.

Variant route

Turn left onto the track and climb gently, passing the picturesque ruins of the **Mas de les Eres** after 10mins. From here the track is easy to follow as it meanders around forested slopes. From time to time the monumental Roques Benet appear to the right, while ahead and to the left there are majestic cliffs and peaks, improbably crowned with pine trees. About 1hr 10mins after the Mas de les Eres the track rises to cross the **Coll de Membrado** and then begins a long descent.

A smaller track turning to the left after 15mins should be ignored in favour of the main track, which now loops to the right to descend close to the **Roques Benet**. After 5mins a cairn marks a small path climbing up to the right onto the Roques. Stay with the main track to pass a signpost some 8mins later and reach a junction where the route forks to the left. After 10mins or so a smaller track

Nearing Arnes, the Roques Benet are seen over an almond plantation

144

comes in on the right; this is where the main route rejoins, some 2hrs after diverging. Continue straight on for a further 15mins to reach a junction with a paved road, where a signpost indicates multiple walking and cycling routes.

Both routes
Turn right onto the road in the direction of Horta Sant Joan, leaving the blue waymarked Estels route and continuing past a signpost for the Salt de Ferrasso (waterfall) after 22mins to reach a junction a few minutes later. Here a green signpost indicates a track to the left for Arnes (5.7km). The way divides after 3mins or so, and keeping to the left the track leads on past well-tended fields of almond and olive trees, backed by the dramatic cliffs of les Gronses and the Moles dels Biarnets. From here the route is plentifully supplied with signposts and the picturesque village of **Arnes** is reached after 1hr 20mins. ▶

Details of recommended hotels in Arnes can be found in Appendix D

Day 2
Leave Arnes by returning along the road walked on day 1, following the signposts for els Estrets and also yellow and white waymarks. Turn right after 40mins at a signposted junction, to leave yesterday's route, onto a track in the direction of els Estrets. The track fords the Estrets river, with concrete stepping stones that are needed when the water is high. Continue straight on after the ford, ignoring a left turn soon after. After 5mins turn right onto a small path marked with a cairn and yellow waymark, leading through the trees and back towards the river. Some 50mins from Arnes the path is joined by the blue waymarked Estels route, fording the river from the right. Afterwards, the route climbs out of the trees to reveal the monumental cliffs of les Gronses ahead and to the left. Down to the right the river of the Estrets re-appears, punctuated by small waterfalls and deep green pools. The way now leads into the dramatic **Estrets d'Arnes**, with sculpted rock slopes on either side. ▶

A sense of mountain grandeur is emphasised by the path being elevated on a terrace above the river.

About half an hour after merging with the Estels route, the path crosses the river on a slender concrete bridge and continues along the opposite bank.

Approaching the Estrets d'Arnes

Leaving the Estrets d'Arnes behind, the character of the walk changes again, as the path enters woodland and winds alongside the Estrets river, now lush and gentle. Along the way signposts confirm the direction for the Area Recreativa de la Franqueta (picnic site), and **La Franqueta** is reached some 2hrs 10mins from the start of the walk. ◀

Drinking water is available here, from taps inside a barbecue shelter.

Leave la Franqueta by the road, turning right to head up river. When it divides after a couple of minutes, take the right fork signposted to **la Marbrera** (ancient marble quarry) and leave the yellow and white waymarks. Another signpost confirms the way soon after and almost immediately the broad path to the quarry can be seen to the left.

Take this path to enter the barranc of the **Carrer Ample** and turn right to walk along the valley bottom. The route now follows the barranc, alternating between stony ground and water-worn rock, with occasional paths diverting from the valley floor to bypass difficult sections. Some 40mins after passing the marble quarry the barranc divides and cairns indicate the route up the right-hand

In the lower, more verdant part of the Carrer Ample

branch. This leads through a verdant section before emerging into an apparently closed rocky amphitheatre although, on closer inspection, the exit is clear. Some 10mins later the path comes to a font and water cistern, reached just over an hour from la Franqueta. From here the barranc climbs steeply to break through a transverse ridge and enter an area of dense woodland.

Leaving the woodland (30mins from the font) the cairned path emerges into a wild and beautiful Karst landscape. A few minutes later it passes a shallow cave and turns a corner to find a way between huge cliffs and climb into a more open area. A subsidiary barranc on the left, passed about 5mins later, has another cave which is sometimes used as a bivouac.

About 20mins after passing the side barranc the path finally leaves the Carrer Ample by making a sharp turn to the right. It climbs the hillside on a cairned path to reach a small rocky ridge and cross an area of open pasture land to join the GR7/Estels path. Here there are red and white and blue waymarks. Making a left turn, the route now continues on to pass the ruined **Mas de Maraco** and

The austere beauty of the upper Carrer Ample

to skirt around a highpoint, before rising onto a ridge as the **Coll d'Alfara** is passed. ▶

The path leaves the ridge to descend through trees and reach the **Coll de l'Enrelojada**, some 30mins after joining the GR7. The col, a small flat grassy space, is marked with a blue starred Estels marker post and an old wooden signpost for Paüls. Here the route turns right on a cairned descent path, waymarked in yellow and white.

This path descends steeply through dense woodland with ample evidence of habitation by wild boar: muddy wallows and signs of rooting. This is the Barranc del Salt, flanked by huge cliffs which can seen from the occasional clearings. The route is clear apart from one junction some 25mins from the col where the path makes a turn to drop to the left. The more obvious route is straight on but a yellow and white cross in this direction confirms the left turn. From here continue descending on the main path following the yellow and white waymarks, ignoring any cairned turns to left or right. After an awkward passage through old terraces and gullies the path arrives at a clearing with a track leading off to the left. After 2mins on this track the yellow and white waymarked path leaves to the right but the route continues along the track.

The track now bends to the left and after 10mins reaches a junction with another track. Turn left here and after approximately 7mins turn right on a descending path waymarked in red and white and marked by a cairn. From now on red and white and blue waymarks indicate the way to Sant Roc. After 5mins the descent eases to reach a junction with the path for the Font de Teix. Keep left on the main path and arrive at a small col of red rock and earth some 8mins later, where there is a junction. Continue straight on and descend gently on a woodland path that gradually becomes a track. Pass several junctions, following the clear waymarking.

Some 12mins later the path reaches the Coll d'en Guasc where the track bends to the left. Here a waymarked path drops to the right to make a shortcut and rejoin the track after 7mins. Turn right to reach **Sant Roc** a minute later, just over an hour from the Coll de l'Enrelojada.

Views now open up across the village of Alfara to the River Ebre.

WALK 26
La Creu de Santos

Difficulty	Route-finding ●● Scrambling ● Exposure ●
Total ascent	550m
Time	3hrs 30mins
Distance	9km
Start	Balneari de Cardó
Maps	Cardó-Rasquera, Editorial Piolet, 1:10,000/1:25,000

For full directions to start, see Appendix B.

The Creu de Santos (cross of the saints) and Xaquera form a double summit on one of the Serra de Cardó's two beautiful ridges. The 360° views from both are outstanding. Being closer to the sea than els Ports, the blue Mediterranean extends out to the east, the Montsia is outlined against the sandy peninsulas and lagoons of the Delta to the south, the length of els Ports stretches out in the west and in winter, far away to the north, the snowy peaks of the Pyrenees can be seen. This circular walk takes in both summits as well as a high ridge walk and three ermitas (hermitages), including one of the most dramatic – perched on its rocky pinnacle.

Leave the parking by the track signposted 'Ermitari de la Vall de Cardó' and after 5mins, where this track bends sharply to the right, continue straight on on a smaller track barred to cars with a chain. The track rises past the ruins of the **Ermita de Sant Simeó**, sometimes called de la Columna, perched on a rocky crag to the left. (To visit this dramatically situated *ermita*, go up the stone steps and follow a small path to the left. Return the same way.) The track narrows to a path and climbs up the Barranc de la Columna. ◄ At a junction some 20mins from the start, at the **Cova dels Porcs**, a tiny metal signpost indicates a left turn for Xaquera. After

Dense vegetation, tall pines and looming cliffs give a tunnel-like feel to this part of the ascent.

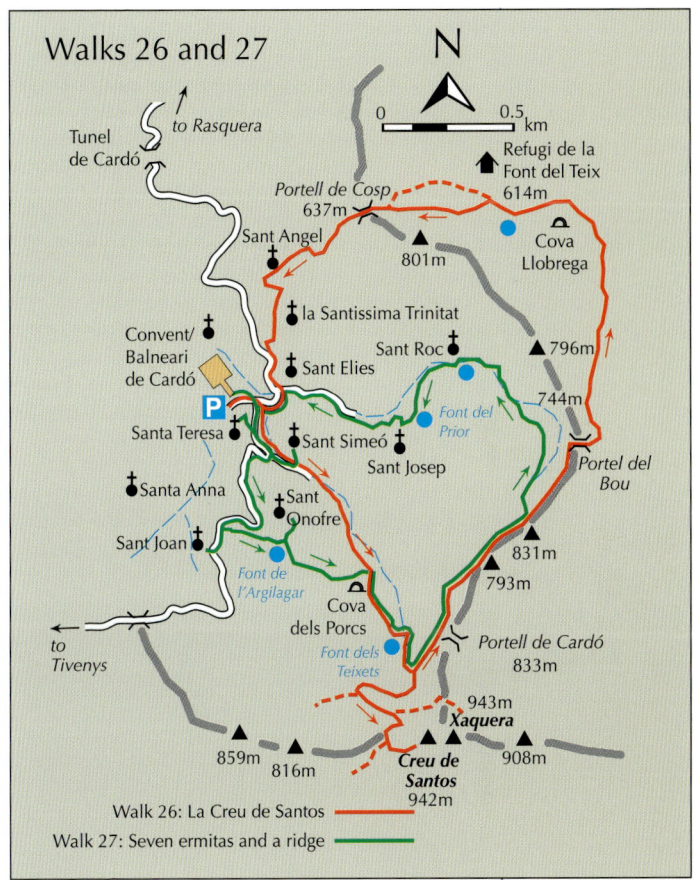

Walks 26 and 27

N

0   0.5 km

to Rasquera

Tunel de Cardó

Portell de Cosp 637m

Refugi de la Font del Teix 614m

Sant Angel

801m

Cova Llobrega

†la Santissima Trinitat

Convent/ Balneari de Cardó

Sant Roc

▲796m

Sant Elies

744m

P

Santa Teresa

Sant Simeó

Fch Font del Prior

Sant Josep

Portel del Bou

Santa Anna

Sant Onofre

Sant Joan

Font de l'Argilagar

831m

793m

Cova dels Porcs

Font dels Teixets

Portell de Cardó 833m

to Tivenys

943m
Xaquera

908m

859m

816m

Creu de Santos 942m

Walk 26: La Creu de Santos

Walk 27: Seven ermitas and a ridge

a further 15mins the path emerges to contour round the base of a cliff which shelters the (now dry) **Font del Teixets**. Here the path climbs over an old rock fall and re-enters woodland, arriving at a T-junction after 3mins or so. The crossing path has yellow waymarks in both directions, and a small metal signpost plate on a rock to the left signposts the three directions. This is the

151

point from which the there-and-back path to the summit starts.

Turning right for Xaquera the path leads steeply up through rocky and wooded terrain. A craggy barrier encountered after 3mins is bypassed by means of an easy rocky gully, recognisable by a makeshift (and unobstructive) animal barrier of wire and netting. At the next junction 10mins later another tiny signpost indicates a left turn for the Creu de Santos. When the path divides again 2mins later, take the right turn for the Creu de Santos, to reach the main Serra ridge 55mins from the start of the walk. The path now crosses the ridge. Ignore a small path to the right with its tiny signpost for the Coll de Murtero and climb to reach the summit of the **Creu de Santos** 10mins later. **Xaquera** is obvious, a little further along the ridge.

Retrace the route back down, through the gully, to the T-junction with the metal plate. From here the route continues on the yellow marked path in the direction signposted to the Font del Teix and Refugi. The path winds northwards through woodland to reach a low point

The route picks its way along the top of the ridge

on a ridge before climbing to a rocky viewpoint, some 1hr 45mins from the start of the walk. ▶ After descending from here for a minute the path reaches a junction with a small metal signpost plate, where another path drops down to the left to the Balneari. Continue straight on for the Font de Teix and Refugi.

The yellow waymarked route now picks its way along the top of the ridge for 15mins, occasionally on a path, until the waymarks lead across the ridge onto its right-hand side at the **Portel del Bou**. Descending on open hillside, the route now splits into many indistinct paths, all of which join a single clear path leading left and undulating below the ridge. Occasional yellow waymarks offer some guidance. Some 40mins after crossing the ridge, the path passes over a small rise with a wooden marker post, its fallen sign for the Refugi i Font de Teix, Portell de Cosp and Rasquera propped up at the base. Continuing over the rise the terrain changes abruptly, from Mediterranean *garrigue* (low and fragrant but thorny scrub) to grass.

The viewpoint offers splendid views over the el Perelló hills and the small coastal resort of l'Ametlla de Mar to the Mediterranean beyond.

CARDÒ – SPAS AND HERMITAGES

At the end of the road from Rasquera, the extensive and romantically decaying buildings of the Balneari de Cardò become visible. The waters of Cardò have long been considered beneficial for health and in 1872 the Balneari opened its doors as a spa and luxury hotel. This lasted until the Civil War, when it was taken over by the Republicans as a hospital. The spa was re-opened and refurbished extensively after the war and operated until the mid-1950s. Several attempts have been made since to renovate the buildings but with limited success. Another initiative is currently taking shape.

The Balneari has an earlier history as the Monastery of Sant Hilari, built in 1604 and followed soon after by the first house and chapel of the Order of the Barefoot Carmelite nuns. The nuns were completely self-sufficient, with their own vegetable gardens, cistern, flour and olive mills, oven and enclosures for animals. The order valued solitude and reflection and built 13 small houses/chapels (ermitas), around the monastery. The ruins of the ermitas, some perched on apparently inaccessible crags, others almost buried in woodland and all with their associated cypress trees, are an enchanting feature of Cardò.

The Ermita de Sant Angel

Pass the **Cova Llobrega** to reach the Font and the **Refugi de la Font del Teix** a few minutes further on. At the refuge ignore the yellow markers leading down to the right and carry straight on along a cairned path which contours the hillside to the left of the valley, through yew trees and old terraces. After descending somewhat the path scrambles up to a large pine tree and crosses consolidated scree before merging with the yellow marked footpath (Cami del Frares). **The Portell de Cosp** is reached by easy zigzags (ignore the unofficial steep gully route with its loose stones). Drop down from this col for 25mins on a clear and easy path which passes through two ruined *ermitas* (look out for the old stables at the second, with the names of the horses still marked) to reach the road. Turn left to regain the start.

WALK 27

Seven ermitas and a ridge

Difficulty	Route-finding ●● Scrambling ●
	Exposure ●
Total ascent	400m
Time	2hrs 50mins
Distance	7km
Start	Balneari de Cardó
Maps	Cardó-Rasquera, Editorial Piolet, 1:10,000/1:25,000
	For route map, see Walk 26.

For full directions to start, see Appendix B.

This circular walk takes place in an area known as the 'Desert of Cardó' and yet walking in it feels much more like a jungle exploration. There is a real sense of discovery about the paths which wind below tall trees and through dense undergrowth to come unexpectedly upon stone chapels and hermitages perched high on the tops of steep cliffs and pinnacles. The route visits four of these extraordinary and ancient places of prayer and contemplation before climbing up through woodland to a high open ridge with airy views and then plunging back into the forest to seek out the remaining three *ermitas*.

Leave the parking by the track signposted 'Ermitari de la Vall de Cardó'. After 3mins the track veers slightly to the right. Look out for an acute right turn by a large pine tree, on a path which begins with three widely spaced stone steps. This is the narrow woodland path that leads to Santa Teresa. It passes through bushes and, after a minute, two rocks with an old metal water pipe running between them can be seen to the right of the path. Approximately 5m further on, turn left onto a trace of a path and climb up to the right of a brick and water pipe construction. About 5mins later the **Ermita de Santa Teresa** is reached, overlooking the Balneari and surrounded by the tall cypress trees which are characteristic of these sites. ▶

The *ermita* was built in 1612 and is fairly well preserved, having been used as living accommodation until comparitively recently.

To continue, descend by the same route to rejoin the track and turn right until, after 2mins, the track bends sharply to the right. Here the route goes straight on, on a smaller track barred to cars with a chain.

This track rises for a minute or so towards the **Ermita de Sant Simeó** (sometimes called la Columna) perched high on a rocky crag above. Stone steps and a small path lead off the track to the left to access this dramatically situated *ermita*. To continue the walk, return to where the chain bars the smaller track and bear left uphill on the main track. After a minute or so a path on the right leads up to a viewpoint offering vistas over the Balneari and the valley below. ◄

On a wooded hillside to the left can be seen the remains of the ancient walls of the monastery and the *ermita* of Santa Anna.

Returning to the track continue uphill for 10mins, to reach a small path leading off to the left and marked with a cairn and a trickle of white paint on a rock. For the moment, continue on past for about 200m, to where a small cairn indicates a path dropping down to the right. This leads quickly to the picturesque ruins of the **Ermita de Sant Joan**, constructed in 1616 and dedicated to St. John the Baptist.

The Ermita de Santa Teresa

The Ermita de Sant Simeó (de la columna)

From the Ermita de Sant Joan return down the track and take the small footpath passed earlier. This climbs into the forest and after 10mins reaches a large stone-built construction known as the **Font de l'Argilagar**. Just before the font the path bears left at a cairn. Some 50m further on there is a junction. The right turn leads to the Cova dels Porcs but, for the moment, turn left onto a path which winds its way out to the rocky spur on which the spectacular **Ermita de Sant Onofre** perches, reached after 10mins.

Return by the same path to the junction and this time carry straight on to reach the **Cova dels Porcs**, some 15mins from Sant Onofre. The 'cova' is not a cave but an undercut cliff with the remains of an enclosure once used to shelter pigs. Just after the cova a junction with a small metal signpost is reached. The left turn leads back to the Balneari but the route now leads straight on in the direction of Xaquera (Creu de Santos), zigzagging up through the woods to the base of a large cliff which can be seen ahead. The path climbs steeply to cross a rockfall and follow round the base of the cliff, passing

157

The Ermita de Sant Onofre

From here there are extensive views out to the Mediterranean near l'Ametlla de Mar.

the (usually dry) **Font del Teixets** some 15mins from the Cova dels Porcs. About 2-3mins later a junction appears. Looking past the yellow marker to the left, a metal plate signpost can be seen. If you wish to climb to the summits of Creu de Santos and Xaquera on the there-and-back path, see Walk 26.

The route turns left here, signposted to the 'Font del Teix and Refugi' along a yellow waymarked path which climbs up for 10mins to reach a ridge. It then continues climbing along it for a further 10mins to its highest point. ◀

The path now drops to the left of the ridge to enter some trees and arrive at a junction 50m beyond the highest point. Turn left to descend on a narrow but clear and cairned path. The path zigzags down towards a forest clearing with a large cairn in its centre and turns right to descend a *barranc*. After 12mins of steeper descent the remains of a *forn de quitra* or pitch oven can be seen to the right; this would have been used for making pitch tar to seal wooden ships. Some 12mins later the **Ermita de Sant Roc** is reached, nestling amongst its cypress trees.

The spring has a working tap and the water is reputed to be therapeutic for skin disorders.

Leave Sant Roc by turning left along the terrace below it, pushing past a cypress tree and then stepping down onto a lower terrace to walk along the terrace wall. From here, the path is overgrown but not difficult to find. Some 10mins after leaving Sant Roc the path reaches another spring, the **Font del Prior**. From here on it becomes obvious that this was once a well-used recreational path through the woods, perhaps by those taking thermal cures to get some gentle exercise and take the waters. There are stone benches all along the route but they are now becoming overgrown, adding to the 'lost' atmosphere of the place. Some 5mins from the Font del Prior, look out for a flight of stone steps leading acutely back to the left. Climbing up here for 20m there is an acute turn to the right onto a small path rising along the top of a stone wall. This climbs past a cave and into a natural grotto, from where steps lead up to the font and **Ermita de Sant Josep**.

To complete the walk, return down the steps to rejoin the main path and continue descending for 5mins to join a grassy track and pass some waterworks constructions. This track leads down to the road in 5mins, passing the sizeable **Ermita de Sant Elies**. Turn left onto the road to pass the Balneari and return to the start.

WALK 28

Mas de Mata-redona

Difficulty	Route-finding ● Scrambling ● Exposure ●
Total ascent	500m plus 110m for extension to la Foradada summit
Time	2hrs 40mins plus 1hr for extension
Distance	8 km plus 3km for extension
Start	Parking in the Barranc de Coll Llarg
Map	Institut Cartografic de Catalunya: 1:50,000 Montsia – gives an overall idea of the topology but lacks footpath detail.

For full directions to start, see Appendix B.

The Montsia ridges have sheltered slopes overlooking the Mediterranean and walking here can often be pleasant when the main els Ports area is cloudy and windy. On this longer Montsia route, the sea is rarely out of sight and there is an optional detour up to the spectacular arch of the Foradada with its remarkable view. The approach by car through the industrial outskirts of Amposta gives little indication of the charm of the walk, which crosses open ridges and passes through tree-filled *barrancs*. Of particular note are the many low-growing fan palms, Europe's only indigenous palm, and the springs and water reservoirs (fonts and cocos).

Looking back over Amposta the road and rail bridges can be seen spanning the ever widening River Ebre, and northwards the coastal views stretch as far as Tarragona.

Continue along the track for 150m, following the red and white markers of the GR92, up to signposts which indicate a left turn onto a small stony path for the 'Itinerari Serra de Montsia' and the 'Pla de Gallos'. The path climbs diagonally up the left flank of the broad *barranc* to gain a dividing ridge after 15mins. Passing over the ridge the views open out across the Delta to the sea beyond. ◄ The path now rises through fragrant low-growing Mediterranean vegetation, with many fan palms. It then passes around the head of a steep wooded valley,

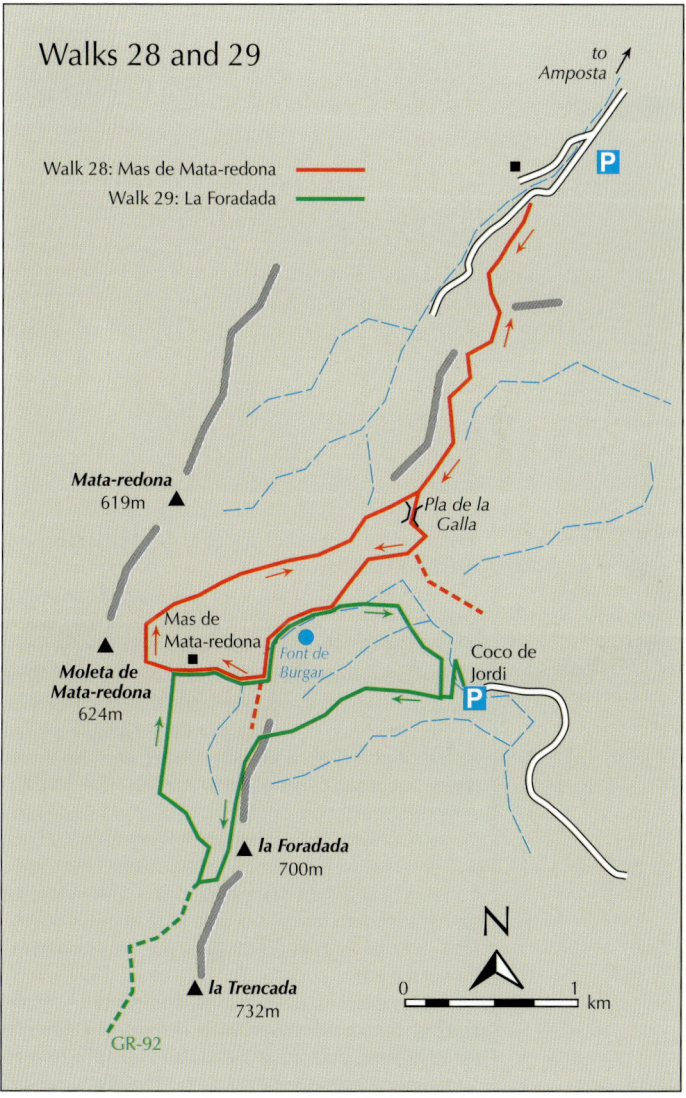

Walks 28 and 29

to
Amposta

Walk 28: Mas de Mata-redona
Walk 29: La Foradada

Mata-redona
619m

Pla de la
Galla

Mas de
Mata-redona

Font de
Burgar

Coco de
Jordi

Moleta de
Mata-redona
624m

la Foradada
700m

la Trencada
732m

GR-92

N

0   1
                        km

Rosemary, lavender and other herbs thrive on the sheltered hillside

staying below the crest of a ridge to the right and making for a broad saddle ahead.

After 10mins or so the path passes a junction with a path on the right, waymarked in red. This is the descent route. Carry straight on to climb gently for 5mins to reach a broad grassy area where old stone walls, terraced fields and a ruined farm building indicate that this was once a cultivated area. This is the **Pla de la Galla**. Look out for the cairn and red and white marker which show the way to a junction of paths and a signpost. Here the route continues straight on, on the GR92 (red and white waymarks), following the sign for the Font del Burgar (850m) and enters a wooded valley noted for its holm oaks. Contouring and then descending below cliffs, the path passes a left turn for the Coco de Jordi and reaches the shady area of the **Font del Burgar** some 50mins from the start of the walk.

Leave the font, following red and white waymarks and the sign for the Mas de Mata-redona, and climb up the right-hand side of a wooded barranc. After 7mins a signposted junction indicates an acute right turn for la

Foradada and the **Mas de Mata-redona**. The extensive and picturesque ruins of the *mas* are reached some 10mins later.

The walk continues through the mas to another signpost where there is an option of going straight on for a there and back route up to la Foradada. This one-hour detour reverses the first section of the descent from the summit in **Walk 29** and is clear and well-signposted.

To continue the circuit, pass through a field immediately by the side of the *mas* in a north-west direction, heading towards a cairn. From here a second cairn can be seen in the same direction, leading out of the field and over a broken down stone wall. A clear, cairned path now leads on to a junction just 2mins from the *mas*. Take the right fork and continue curving around above the Mas de Mata-redona to settle into an easterly direction (towards the sea), effectively paralleling the outward route on a higher level. A standing stone, reached 25mins from the *mas*, marks the beginning of the descent from the ridge. Head down for 25mins to reach a junction with a tiny wooden signpost. Turn left here and follow the red markers to descend through an area of old terraces to reach the GR92 after some 4mins. This completes the circuit and a left turn retraces the ascent to reach the start 30mins later.

WALK 29
La Foradada

Difficulty	Route-finding ● Scrambling ● Exposure ●
Total ascent	400m
Time	2hrs 15mins
Distance	5km
Start	Coco de Jordi
Map	Institut Cartografic de Catalunya: 1:50,000 Montsia; gives an overall idea of the topology but lacks footpath detail
	For route map, see Walk 28.

For full directions to start, see Appendix B.

This is an easy circular walk on the sheltered Mediterranean-facing slopes of the Serra de Montsia, on well-marked paths. A steep rocky path climbs quickly up to the spectacular arch of the Foradada. The descent is gentle, passing a ruined *mas* before winding down a shady barranc, complete with springs and the ruins of a limekiln.

Leave the car park by the footpath signed for la Foradada and waymarked in yellow and white. Very soon turn right at a crossroads, leading on to another signpost. The route now takes the smaller of the footpaths, leading straight ahead and signposted for la Rueda and la Foradada. This unmarked path climbs steeply and more or less directly up the hillside towards the ridge. There are no waymarks but it is easy to see on the ground. After 30mins or so a small post with a green diamond on its top marks a junction with a wider path joining from the right. This is the PR83 and here the route turns left to follow its yellow and white waymarks.

A broad ridge is reached some 15mins later, offering 360° views. ◀ The fishing port of Sant Carles de la Rapita

Ahead is the rocky outline of the Foradada.

164

spreads to the left below, and beyond it is the huge curving sandbank of la Banya, enclosing the bay of Alfacs. Over to the right stretches the Serra de Godall and the els Ports massif. After walking along the ridge for 12mins or so there is a signpost which marks the final climb up to **La Foradada**. Its estimate of 2mins is encouraging but ambitious. Several steep minutes bring the reward – a deep, rocky arch with views across the Delta to the sea beyond.

The descent begins by continuing on past the archway, following the yellow and white waymarks down to another signpost at a crossroads of paths. Turn right (signposted Mata-redona 1120m) to follow the red and white markers of the GR92 and descend more steeply towards the ruined **Mas de Mata-redona** which can be seen below. These picturesque ruins are reached some 25mins after starting the descent.

A signpost for the Font del Burgar and the Coco de Jordi indicates the path through the *mas* and a red and white waymark on the corner of one of the buildings shows the onward direction. Now the route enters trees and winds its way on a well-made path down a valley

La Foradada

Looking down on Sant Carles de la Rapita from the ridge

alongside a (mostly) dry stream bed to reach the shady springs of the **Font del Burgar** some 20mins later. Follow the signpost for Coco de Jordi along a path with both red and white and yellow and white waymarks. After 5mins the two paths diverge. Take the descending path to the right (signposted for Coco de Jordi), the yellow and white marked PR83. After 3mins it passes the substantial remains of an old limekiln and from here leads easily and clearly back to the start.

WALK 30
Coastal path

Difficulty	Route-finding ● Scrambling ● Exposure ●
Total ascent	approx 250m
Time	4hrs 45mins
Distance	17km
Start	Train station, l'Ametlla de Mar
Map	Institut Cartografic de Catalunya, 1:50,000 Baix Ebre gives an overall idea of the topology but lacks footpath detail

For full directions to start, see Appendix B.

The stretch of coastline between the small coastal towns of l'Ametlla de Mar and l'Ampolla is a delightfully undeveloped series of low cliffs, inaccessible coves and small sandy bays. The GR92 coastal path winds up and down to follow the edge of the sea as closely as possible, sometimes crossing beaches, sometimes weaving into the olive groves to negotiate creeks. Since the railway joins the two towns, it is possible to leave a car at l'Ampolla and travel by train to l'Ametlla so as to walk the whole stretch. Alternatively there-and-back walks can be made from either end, or from the Platja de l'Aliga, where there is road access.

From the **l'Ametlla de Mar** railway station turn right and then left past the park to walk directly down through the town to the fishing harbour. Turn right to walk along the sea front, and look for a set of steps to climb up onto a higher level overlooking the yacht harbour. At the end of the harbour there is a noticeboard marking the **Cala Pepo** and the start of the walk. Red and white markers indicate a path dropping down into the next bay.

After 20mins the path reaches a headland just before a deeply indented creek, marked with a lighthouse. This is the Port de l'Estany and to negotiate it the route turns

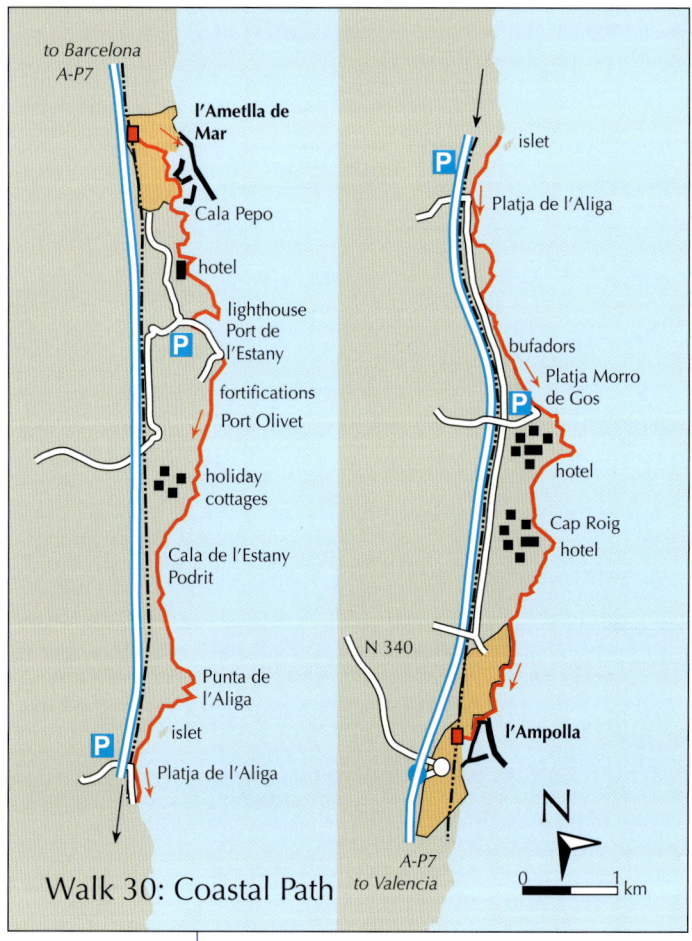

Walk 30: Coastal Path

right to go inland. Soon after turning there is a red and white marker on a telephone pole. At the end of this stony track turn left onto a small road. Continue on this road, following the red and white marker and ignoring a turn to the left. At the next junction turn left, following the sign for **Port Olivet**. The route now enters an area of old coastal military installations which are well-signposted.

Leaving the military installations behind, continue on the path, dropping in and out of coves and crossing beaches until, some 1hr 20mins from the start, it reaches a group of stone-built holiday cottages. Follow the clear red and white waymarks across the broad Estany Podrit bay and around the rocky **Punta de l'Aliga** headland from where a picturesque rocky islet can be seen ahead.

After passing the islet the path comes down into the next cove, where the route is not obvious. Continue across the cove to its far end where steps can be seen leading up to the right. They lead to a house but just before the last steps a red and white marker indicates a path leading off to the left. A few minutes later the wide **Platja de l'Aliga** beach is reached, some 2hrs 45mins from the start of the walk. There is road access to this point of the walk.

From the Platja l'Aliga take the concrete road up to just past a barrier, where a substantial but unmarked

The rocky islet after the Punta de l'Aliga

The path dips past one of the many coves

footpath turns to the left. Ignore the very numerous and brightly painted red and white markers which offer an alternative route on the road alongside the railway. That would bypass a lovely, albeit slightly exposed, section of coastal path around a headland. Follow the footpath, with its wooden handrail, along the top of the cliffs. A few minutes later the path joins a track; turn left to drop down into the next bay and walk along the beach alongside a sea wall of large stone blocks. Where this wall is interrupted by a gully, turn right into the gully for a few metres to find a small path climbing up to the left. This path continues to rise in the same direction through scrubby vegetation for just under a minute before turning right to climb up to the foot of some cliffs. A sharp left turn then leads out onto the headland.

The path is clear on the ground as it scrambles up and down short rocky sections but the red and white markers are very worn and infrequent. Some 12mins from the gully the path climbs a little and enters an area of stone terrace walls, following the edge of one of the terraces. An old red and white waymark on a rock on the right indicates a right-angle turn to the right to climb up on steps to the next level of terrace and continue ascending slightly along it to where some stone steps drop down to the terrace below. Turn left down the steps then continue to descend on further steps and cross the rock below to find a path continuing around the headland at a slightly lower level. This path leads across sloping rocks and down into the next cove, some 25mins from the Platja de l'Aliga.

From the cove cross a small gully and climb up steeply through trees, where the newly painted red and white markers are re-encountered, leading in from the alternative road route. The path continues to be well marked from this point on as it winds through trees and then drops down to the shore by a flight of steps just before a house, some 10mins after leaving the last cove. ▶ The route follows the shoreline, or alternatively along wooden ramping, leading to a car park and road, arriving at the broad **Platja Morro de Gos** beach and signpost some 50mins from the Platja de l'Aliga.

This stretch of shoreline is formed from ancient coral and the sea finds channels under it to surge into rock pools or bufadors.

Looking back from the Platja del Baconé, close to l'Ampolla

There is a small café here but it is not often open during the winter months.

At this point you can continue on the road or on the beach. ◄ Climb the steps at the end of the bay then either drop into the next bay (Cala de Buena) and climb out again or skirt around the top of the bay on a concrete road. Both join a well-made jogging track that curves around a modern hotel built on a headland. Some 10mins from the Platja Morro de Gos look out for a small concrete path descending to the left from some flat scrubland. A red and white marker confirms the route a little way down. The well waymarked path now continues climbing and descending into a series of bays until it reaches the main **Cap Roig** headland with another hotel, some 30mins from the Platja Morro de Gos.

Now the path hugs the coastline, reaching the suburbs of l'Ampolla after about 20mins, at the broad Platja del Baconé. The route joins the road briefly before turning left along a path barred against traffic by some large rocks. This path soon joins a road which leads into **l'Ampolla** and the railway station.

Looking back from near Cap Roig

THE COAST

The waters off the local coast have always been rich in sea-life, partly because there is a wide underwater shelf ideal for fish to breed, but mainly because the Ebre river brings down nutrients that support an abundance of plankton and other micro-organisms to feed a wide variety of fish and shell-fish. Fishermen created the first small coastal settlements in the 16th century, at both l'Ampolla and l'Ametlla de Mar; and fishing is still important in both villages today. Sardines, tuna, anchovies, monkfish, hake, red mullet, sea bass, bream, squid and octopus are landed regularly and can be seen at the afternoon auctions in both places. Just south of l'Ampolla in the bay of Fangar there are oyster beds, while offshore mussel farms can be seen from the coastal walk south of l'Ametlla. It is therefore not surprising that the local restaurants offer a wide range of seafood.

The substantial stretch of coast between the two villages is designated an area of special natural (biological) interest for its seaweed fields and for an endemic snail, giving overall protection to its natural beauty.

More information can be found at www.ampolla.org and www.ametllademar.org.

(inset) The fishing port of l'Ampolla

APPENDIX A
Route summary table

No	Walk	Ascent (m)	Time	Distance (km)	Route-finding	Scrambling	Exposure	Page
1	Punta de l'Aigua	900	4h30	13	●●	●●	●●	37
2	Montaspre ridge	750	3h40	13	●●	●	●●	43
3	Moleta de les Canals: circuit	750	4h	11	●●●	●●	●●	48
	summit ridge	650	3h20	8				
4	Barranc del Camp	370	2h	10	●	●	●	55
5	Solana route	700	4h15	14	●●	●●	●●	58
6	Cova dels Adells	325	1h25	5	●	●	●	64
7	Coll d'en Caubet and Valliguera	850	4h15	12	●●	●	●	66
8	Cervera and Figuera valleys: circuit	270	2h30	10	●●	●●	●●	70
	extension	225	2h30	5				
9	La Moleta	460	2h20	6	●	(●● optional)	● (●●● optional)	76
10	Vall d'Infern: circuit	320	1h40	5	●	●●	●●	79
	extension	140	0h45	2				
11	Pi del Perillo	140	1h20	5	●	●	●	82
12	Mont Caro summit	650	3h30	7	●●●	●●●	●●	84
13	Mola del Moro	550	3h40	8	●●●	●●	(●●● optional)	90
14	La Barcina	80	1h5	3	●	●	●	96

No	Walk	Ascent (m)	Time	Distance (km)	Route-finding	Scrambling	Exposure	Page
15	Cresta del Marturi	650	4h20	12	••	•	••	98
16	Sources of the Matarranya	530	3h30	16	••	•	•	103
17	Roca del Migdia	800	5h	12	•••	•••	•••	109
18	Caramella gorge	250	2h	3	•	•••	•••	116
19	Mola Castellona	800	4h15	10	••	••	••	119
20	Lloret high level route	1000	6h	17	••	••	••	123
21	Barranc de Lloret	150	1h50	4	•	•	•	128
22	Roca Xapada	550	2h15	6	•	•	••	130
23	Font del Paradis	540	3h20	10	•	•	•	133
24	Coll de Lloret	300	1h45	6	•	•	•	137
25	Sant Roc to Arnes and back: Day 1 main route	700	5h45	22	••	••	•••	139
	Day 1 variant	650	5h20	26	•	•••		
	Day 2	750	6h15	25	••	•		
26	La Creu de Santos	550	3h30	9	••	•	•	150
27	Seven ermitas and a ridge	400	2h50	7	••	•	•	155
28	Mas de Mata-redona: circuit	500	2h40	8	••	••	••	160
	extension	110	1h	3				
29	La Foradada	400	2h15	5	•	••	••	164
30	Coastal path	250	4h45	17	•	•	•	167

APPENDIX B
Finding the walks

Finding the starts of some of the walks can be an adventure in itself. The access routes are unclear on the available maps and poorly signposted, if at all. The approximate locations of the starts are shown on the Location of Walks map, for use in conjunction with the detailed directions given here. All the walk starts can be reached by a conventional road vehicle, although two are on tracks where a less than average ground clearance could be a problem: the approach to la Caramella (Walks 17–19); and the Caro–Fredes track (Walk 16). Both have some particularly rough sections.

To Paüls (Walks 1 and 2)
Take the C12 north from Tortosa, on the true right bank of the River Ebre. After 14km take the junction on the right signed for Xerta and Paüls (this is the third junction for Xerta). At the T-junction at the end of the exit road turn right for Paüls on the TV3541, reached after 9km. For Walk 1 take the right turn just before entering the village, at the huge village name-plate and climb a narrow road which zigzags to reach the Placa Major. Parking can usually be found here. Alternatively, follow the directions for the start of the walk and park near the cemetery. For Walk 2 continue on into the village and park in the short main street.

To Sant Roc (Walks 3, 4 and 25)
Pass the huge village name plate of Paüls, continue on to the entrance of the village and turn left into the small

road signed to Sant Roc. There is ample parking at Sant Roc.

To el Toscar (Walks 5–7)
Take the T-341 west from Tortosa through Roquetes, in the direction of els Reguers and Alfara de Carles. After passing through els Reguers continue for approximately 7km until the road takes a sweeping bend to the right and then, at the apex of the bend, turn left onto the small road signposted el Tosca. After some 4.5km the road enters the hamlet of el Toscar and the parking place is immediately below an electricity substation, by an information board which details the Cova dels Adells route (Walk 6).

To La Peixera de la Flor (Walk 8)
Take the T-341 west from Tortosa through Roquetes, in the direction of els Reguers and Alfara de Carles. Pass through els Reguers and take a left

turn immediately before the irrigation canal to drive along its side. Turn first right to cross the canal and find a narrow road which leads to a hamlet of weekend chalets, known as La Peixera de la Flor. After 2.5km and before the hamlet, where a small road leads down to the left, there is space to park the car. Some 50m further on there is a second junction with a similar parking space.

To the Bassa d'Ossera and Font Nova (Walks 9–11)

Take the C12 north from Tortosa, along the true right bank of the River Ebre. After 12km, approaching Xerta, look for a picnic site on the right. Almost immediately afterwards there is a stop sign on the left, where a narrow road joins. Make an acute left turn onto it and follow it round many bends to reach a T-Junction after 4km, at the irrigation canal. Turn left and then immediately turn right to cross the canal onto its opposite side. Turn left after about 50m onto the narrow road towards the Bassa d'Ossera and Font Nova. Continue for another 1.5km until you reach an obvious car park by the Bassa d'Ossera (Walk 11). For Font Nova for Walks 9 and 10 continue on for a further 2km, to the end of the road.

To the Caro massif (Walks 12–16)

Take the T-341 west from Tortosa through Roquetes, in the direction of els Reguers and Alfara de Carles. At 2km from Roquetes turn left at a substantial junction onto a smaller road signposted for Caro. This leads through a new suburban development and then on up the mountain for nearly 20km. For la Barcina (Walk 14) and the Coll de Vicari (Walks 12 and 13) turn left onto the road to the Caro summit, approximately 1km after the road levels out. After approximately 2km the road bends sharply to the right and the start of Walk 14 is marked with a signpost and an itinerary board. There is space here to park off the road. For Walks 12 and 13 continue on to where the road reaches the main mountain ridge. Park anywhere where the car can be tucked off the road between here and the summit.

For the Coll de Carrasqueta (Walk 15) pass the Caro summit turning and continue on through the hamlet of l'Esquirol on its only principal road, until a clear junction is reached. This is the Coll de Carrasqueta, where a signboard recommends continuation by 4x4 vehicle. There is ample roadside parking here. For the Caro–Fredes track (Walk 16) ignore the 4x4 recommendation and bear left in the direction of Fredes on a mostly unsurfaced and often rough track, passable, with care, in a conventional car. After 3km pass the turning for the Cova Avellanes and at 5km there is good parking, where a track joins on the left.

To the Casa de Carvallo in la Caramella (Walks 17–19)

Take the T-341 west from Tortosa through Roquetes, in the direction of els Reguers and Alfara de Carles. At 2km from Roquetes turn left at a substantial junction onto a smaller road signposted for Caro and then, after a further 2km, cross the irrigation canal and turn left onto a small road some 50m further on. Follow this to its end at a T-junction, after nearly 4km. Turn left here and then immediately right, by a green sign which once said 'Cami de la Caramella'. Follow this track, rough in places, for a little over 2km to its end at the Casa de Carvallo. There is ample parking space by the Casa.

To the Barranc de Lloret (Walks 20 and 21)

From Tortosa cross the River Ebre on the new(ish) Pont del Mil-lenari and continue straight on at the roundabout, through Raval de Crist to another roundabout. Take the third exit (left) for the village of Mas de Barberans, on the TV-3421. After passing the km19 post look for the next turn on the right, signposted 'Barranc de Lloret'. The narrow road winds into the mountains, passing the corrals and buildings of bull farms. Signs warn of the wild bulls (*Bous Braus*), sometimes encountered meandering in the road. After 6km the road ends and there is space for parking here.

To the Racó d'en Marc and la Vall (Walks 22–24)

From Tortosa cross the River Ebre on the new(ish) Pont del Mil-lenari and continue straight on at the roundabout, through Raval de Crist to another roundabout. Take the third exit (left) for the village of Mas de Barberans, on the TV-3421. Go through Mas de Barberans and continue on for a further 3km, then take a small road on the right signposted for 'Cami del Barranc de la Galera and la Vall'. Follow the surfaced road ignoring junctions with tracks. After a bridge the road itself becomes an unsurfaced track and continues on without junctions until, after 5.5 km from the TV-3421, the entrance to the Racó d'en Marc (Walk 22) is reached. Here a wooden footbridge crosses the *barranc* and there is off-track parking by an information board. For la Vall (Walks 23 and 24) continue on for a further 0.5km, where a junction to the left signed for 'Area de Lleure de la Vall' (the picnic site) leads downhill to the parking.

To the Balneari de Cardó (Walks 26 and 27)

Take the C12 north from Tortosa, on the true right bank of the River Ebre. After 30km take the junction on the right signed for Rasquera, el Perelló and l'Ametlla de Mar. Ignore the left turn for el Perelló and continue on to take a left turn into the village, about 1km from the C12. After a few hundred metres bear left uphill at a junction marked by a small monument painted up rather like a marquee. This narrow and scenic road ends 9km later at the Balneari de Cardó. There is a good parking area here, adjacent to the Balneari and the (now closed) water bottling plant.

To the Serra del Montsia (Walks 28 and 29)

From Tortosa cross the River Ebre on the new(ish) Pont del Mil-lenari to the true right bank and turn left at the roundabout onto the C12 for Amposta. Follow this for 17km to its end south of Amposta, passing through three further roundabout junctions and then join the N340 in the direction of Valencia. For the Barranc de Coll Llarg (Walk 28), after passing the km1078 post make a right turn onto a small road. There is a green signpost at the entrance to the road, just before some derelict chicken sheds which reads 'la Vall Llobrega GR 92 parking' but it is not easy to see from the main road. Continue straight on, ignoring all side tracks, through citrus and almond plantations. At a junction just after a factory building bear left on the now deteriorating road. There is parking approximately 2.5km from the N340 by the side of a newly-made wall on the left.

For the Coco de Jordi (Walk 29), continue on the N340 past the km1073 post and turn right at a small crossroads approximately 0.5km further on. A few metres from the junction there is a pale green signpost on the right for the 'Cami de Mata-redona, Area Interpretativa del bosc de Burgar and La Foradada'. Follow this narrow road for 3km to the car park at its end, at the Coco de Jordi.

Coastal Path (Walk 30)

At the time of writing there are nine trains a day from Tortosa to L'Ametlla. Realistically the usable ones are 0748, 0918 and 1045, with a journey time of 30mins. All call at l'Ampolla approximately 15mins after leaving Tortosa. There are 10 return trains from l'Ampolla to Tortosa with the most useful at 1523, 1659, 1828 and 2007, all of which call at l'Ametlla approximately 10mins earlier.

APPENDIX C

Catalan–English glossary of mountain terms

This glossary will help you interpret features on the recommended maps.

aigua	water
aiguamolls	marshes
avenc	pothole
barranc	ravine (dictionary) but also used for (mostly) dry water courses and associated valleys
bassa, bassis	reservoir
bosc	wood, forest
cami	track
clot	pasture
coco	cistern, reservoir
coll	saddle, col
cova	cave with horizontal entrance
cresta	ridge
escarrisó, escaleta	ladder
estrets	narrows
faig	beech tree
faixes	cliffs
foies	moist grassy hollows
font	spring
forat, foradada	rock arch
gubies	very narrow, water-worn passages between tall cliffs
mas	farm
masia	farm house
mola, moles, moleta	mountains with flat tops
montsagre	sacred mountain
ombria, ombries	north-facing or shady slopes
pi	pine tree
pla	flat area
plana	plain
pou	well or cistern
port	gateway
punta	peak
racó	special corner or place
riera	stream
riu	river
roca, roques	rock, rocks
salt	waterfall
serra	mountain group
solana	south-facing or sunny slope
teix	yew tree
toll	water-formed rock basin
tossa, tossal	hill
vall	valley

APPENDIX D
Useful contacts

Transport

Getting there
- Flights to Reus airport by Ryanair, www.ryanair.com
- Flights to Barcelona airport by Easyjet, www.easyjet.com, Jet2, www.Jet2.com or British Airways, www.britishairways.com
- Rail travel from UK by Rail Europe, www.raileurope.co.uk
- Rail travel in Spain by Renfe, www.renfe.es
- Bus travel from UK by Eurolines, www.eurolines.com
- Bus travel in Catalunya by HIFE, www.hife.es

Taxis in Tortosa
- Parada de Taxis, Poeta Vicent Garcia, tel. 0034 977 44 30 11
- Taxis Felip, tel. 0034 977 44 26 09, mobile 0034 609 447 852
- Taxis Juan Trigo, mobile 0034 610 334 245
- Taxis Serret, tel. 0034 977 50 11 64, mobile 0034 617 300 135

Accommodation

Hotels
Most hotels in Tortosa can be viewed and booked online at www.booking.com
- Suda Castle Parador Hotel ****, Tortosa, 0034 977 44 44 50 www.parador.es
- Hotel Rural Panxampla, Carretera d'Alfara, els Reguers, 0034 977 47 41 35 www.elcellerdenpanxampla.com
- Hotel Pepo, Carrer Piscines 1, Benifallet, 0034 977 46 22 00 www.hotelpepo.com
- Hotel Spa Villa Retiro*****, Carrer dels Molins 2, Xerta, 0034 977 47 30 03 www.hotelvillaretiro.com
- Vilar Rural dels Ports, Arnes, 0034 977 43 57 37 www.vilarsrurals.com
- Can Barrina Sta Madrona 27, Arnes, 0034 977 43 51 37 www.canbarrina.net

Rental Properties and B&Bs
English-run rental properties and B&Bs in Tortosa, Roquetes, Raval de Jesus, els Reguers, Benifallet, Aldover and Alfara de Carles can be viewed and booked through:
- Ebro Tours, www.ebrotours.co.uk, tel. 0034 977 26 73 82

- Brighter Spain, www.brighterspain.com, tel. 0034 619 77 24 92
- Owners Direct, www.ownersdirect.co.uk
- Ebro River Rentals, www.ebroriverrentals.com
- Village accommodation in Paüls, Xerta, Mas de Barberans Alfara de Carles and Benifallet can be viewed on www.terresdelebre.com.

Refuges

els Ports, close to walks:
- Refugi de Caro (Walks 12–16), guardian in summer and occasional weekends (tel. 0034 977 26 71 28), no water.
- Refugi de Font Nova (Walks 9–11), key needed in advance (tel. 0034 977 47 36 64).
- Refugi de les Clotes (Walks 5 and 7), unguarded, no water.

els Ports vicinity:
- Refugi de Fontferrera, guardian in summer and weekends, water also available at other times (tel. 0034 977 26 71 10).
- Refugi del Mas del Frare, key needed in advance (tel. 0034 630 518 254).

Cardó:
- Refugi de la Font del Teix in the Cardó (Walk 26), unguarded but well appointed, water nearby. Open all year.

Other mountain accommodation

- Restaurant del Port at l'Esquirol (near walks 12–16) near Mont Caro (tel. 0034 977 26 71 43) has rooms but its opening times are whimsical.
- Residencia Casa de Pages 'Ca les Barberes' at Paüls (tel. 0034 977 43 56 29) offers year-round hostel type accommodation.

Natural Park Information Centres

- Parc Natural dels Ports Centre of Informacion, Avenida Val de Zafan, 43520 Roquetes, tel. 0034 977 50 08 45 or www.gencat.cat, select els Ports.
- Parc Natural del Delta de l'Ebre, Ecomuseu, Carrer Doctor Marti Buera 22, 43580 Deltebre, tel. 0034 977 48 96 79 and Casa de Fusta (exhibition centre), Partida de la Cuixota, 43870 Poble Nou del Delta, tel. 0034 977 26 10 22 or www.gencat.cat, select Delta de l'Ebre.

Tourist Offices and Websites

- Tortosa Tourist Office, Plaça del Carrilet 1, 43500 Tortosa, tel. 0034 977 44 96 48; www.turismetortosa.cat/en

- Regional tourist website (no public office) www.terresdelebre.com

Guided Excursions
- Guided mountain walking trips (English-speaking) can be organised through Ebro Tours, www.ebrotours.com.
- Guided bird-watching walks (English-speaking) are offered by www.ebrotours.co.uk and www.andouinbirding.com.

Maps
- Maps and other publications can be puchased from the main Tortosa bookshop: Llibreria la2 de Viladrich, Carrer Cristòfol Despuig 22.
- Maps can usually be obtained from the Parc Natural dels Ports Centre of Information, Avenida Val de Zafan, 43520 Roquetes, tel. 0034 977 50 08 45.
- Publications can be ordered online from the bookshop at www.la2deviladrich.cat/public/en, which has an English language option, or from www.editorialpiolet.com (Catalan only).

NOTES

NOTES

NOTES

NOTES

LISTING OF CICERONE GUIDES

BRITISH ISLES CHALLENGES, COLLECTIONS AND ACTIVITIES

The End to End Trail
The Mountains of England and Wales
Vol 1: Wales
Vol 2: England
The National Trails
The Relative Hills of Britain
The Ridges of England, Wales and Ireland
The UK Trailwalker's Handbook
Three Peaks, Ten Tors
Unjustifiable Risk? A social history of climbing
World Mountain Ranges: Scotland

NORTHERN ENGLAND TRAILS

A Northern Coast to Coast Walk
Backpacker's Britain: Northern England
Hadrian's Wall Path
The Dales Way
The Pennine Way
The Spirit of Hadrian's Wall

LAKE DISTRICT

An Atlas of the English Lakes
Coniston Copper Mines
Great Mountain Days in the Lake District
Lake District Winter Climbs
Roads and Tracks of the Lake District
Rocky Rambler's Wild Walks
Scrambles in the Lake District North & South
Short Walks in Lakeland
Book 1: South Lakeland
Book 2: North Lakeland
Book 3: West Lakeland
The Central Fells
The Cumbria Coastal Way
The Cumbria Way and the Allerdale Ramble
The Lake District Anglers' Guide
The Mid-Western Fells
The Near Eastern Fells
The Southern Fells
The Tarns of Lakeland
Vol 1: West
Vol 2: East
Tour of the Lake District

NORTH WEST ENGLAND AND THE ISLE OF MAN

A Walker's Guide to the Lancaster Canal
Historic Walks in Cheshire
Isle of Man Coastal Path
The Isle of Man
The Ribble Way
Walking in Lancashire
Walking in the Forest of Bowland and Pendle
Walking on the West Pennine Moors
Walks in Lancashire Witch Country
Walks in Ribble Country
Walks in Silverdale and Arnside
Walks in The Forest of Bowland

NORTH EAST ENGLAND, YORKSHIRE DALES AND PENNINES

Historic Walks in North Yorkshire
South Pennine Walks
The Cleveland Way and the Yorkshire Wolds Way
The North York Moors
The Reivers Way
The Teesdale Way
The Yorkshire Dales Angler's Guide
The Yorkshire Dales:
North and East
South and West
Walking in County Durham
Walking in Northumberland
Walking in the North Pennines
Walking in the Wolds
Walks in Dales Country
Walks in the Yorkshire Dales
Walks on the North York Moors Books 1 & 2

DERBYSHIRE, PEAK DISTRICT AND MIDLANDS

High Peak Walks
Historic Walks in Derbyshire
The Star Family Walks
Walking in Derbyshire
White Peak Walks:
The Northern Dales
The Southern Dales

SOUTHERN ENGLAND

A Walker's Guide to the Isle of Wight
London: The Definitive Walking Guide
The Cotswold Way
The Greater Ridgeway
The Lea Valley Walk
The North Downs Way
The South Downs Way
The South West Coast Path
The Thames Path
Walking in Bedfordshire
Walking in Berkshire
Walking in Buckinghamshire
Walking in Kent
Walking in Sussex
Walking in the Isles of Scilly
Walking in the Thames Valley
Walking on Dartmoor

WALES AND WELSH BORDERS

Backpacker's Britain: Wales
Glyndwr's Way
Great Mountain Days in Snowdonia
Hillwalking in Snowdonia
Hillwalking in Wales Vols 1 & 2
Offa's Dyke Path
Ridges of Snowdonia
Scrambles in Snowdonia
The Ascent of Snowdon
The Lleyn Peninsula Coastal Path
The Pembrokeshire Coastal Path
The Shropshire Hills
The Spirit Paths of Wales
Walking in Pembrokeshire
Walking on the Brecon Beacons
Welsh Winter Climbs

SCOTLAND

Backpacker's Britain:
Central and Southern Scottish Highlands
Northern Scotland
Ben Nevis and Glen Coe
Border Pubs and Inns
North to the Cape
Not the West Highland Way
Scotland's Best Small Mountains

IRELAND

Irish Coastal Walks
The Irish Coast to Coast Walk
The Mountains of Ireland

ITALY

Central Apennines of Italy
Gran Paradiso
Italian Rock
Italy's Sibillini National Park
Shorter Walks in the Dolomites
Through the Italian Alps
Trekking in the Apennines
Treks in the Dolomites
Via Ferratas of the Italian Dolomites: Vols 1 & 2
Walking in Sicily
Walking in the Central Italian Alps
Walking in the Dolomites
Walking in Tuscany
Walking on the Amalfi Coast

MEDITERRANEAN

Jordan – Walks, Treks, Caves, Climbs and Canyons
The Ala Dag
The High Mountains of Crete
The Mountains of Greece
Treks & Climbs in Wadi Rum, Jordan
Walking in Malta
Western Crete

NORTH AMERICA

British Columbia
The Grand Canyon
The John Muir Trail
The Pacific Crest Trail

SOUTH AMERICA

Aconcagua and the Southern Andes
Torres del Paine

SCANDINAVIA

Trekking in Greenland
Walking in Norway

SLOVENIA, CROATIA AND MONTENEGRO

The Julian Alps of Slovenia
The Mountains of Montenegro
Trekking in Slovenia
Walking in Croatia

SPAIN AND PORTUGAL

Costa Blanca Walks
Vol 1: West
Vol 2: East
Mountain Walking in Southern Catalunya
The Mountains of Central Spain
Trekking through Mallorca
Via de la Plata
Walking in Madeira
Walking in Mallorca
Walking in the Algarve
Walking in the Canary Islands
Vol 2: East
Walking in the Cordillera Cantabrica
Walking in the Sierra Nevada
Walking the GR7 in Andalucia
Walks and Climbs in the Picos de Europa

SWITZERLAND

Alpine Pass Route
Central Switzerland
The Bernese Alps
Tour of the Jungfrau Region
Walking in the Valais
Walking in Ticino
Walks in the Engadine

EUROPEAN CYCLING

Cycle Touring in France
Cycle Touring in Ireland
Cycle Touring in Spain
Cycle Touring in Switzerland
Cycling in the French Alps
Cycling the Canal du Midi
Cycling the River Loire
The Danube Cycleway
The Grand Traverse of the Massif Central
The Way of St James Cyclist Guide

TECHNIQUES

Indoor Climbing
Map and Compass
Mountain Weather
Moveable Feasts
Outdoor Photography
Rock Climbing
Snow and Ice Techniques
Sport Climbing
The Book of the Bivvy
The Hillwalker's Guide to Mountaineering
The Hillwalker's Manual

MINI GUIDES

Avalanche!
Navigating with a GPS
Navigation
Pocket First Aid and Wilderness Medicine
Snow

For full and up-to-date information on our ever-expanding list of guides, visit our website: **www.cicerone.co.uk**.

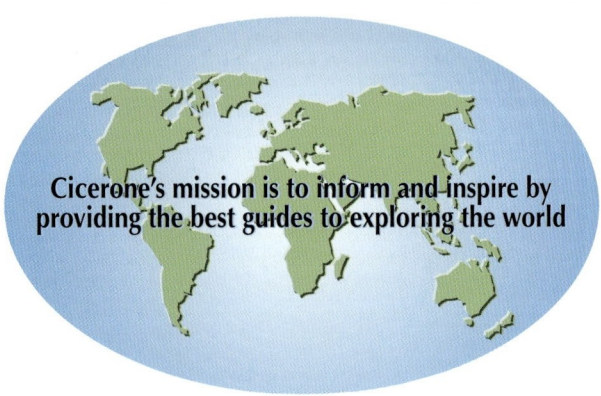

Cicerone's mission is to inform and inspire by providing the best guides to exploring the world

Since its foundation 40 years ago, Cicerone has specialised in publishing guidebooks and has built a reputation for quality and reliability. It now publishes nearly 300 guides to the major destinations for outdoor enthusiasts, including Europe, UK and the rest of the world.

Written by leading and committed specialists, Cicerone guides are recognised as the most authoritative. They are full of information, maps and illustrations so that the user can plan and complete a successful and safe trip or expedition – be it a long face climb, a walk over Lakeland fells, an alpine cycling tour, a Himalayan trek or a ramble in the countryside.

With a thorough introduction to assist planning, clear diagrams, maps and colour photographs to illustrate the terrain and route, and accurate and detailed text, Cicerone guides are designed for ease of use and access to the information.

If the facts on the ground change, or there is any aspect of a guide that you think we can improve, we are always delighted to hear from you.

Cicerone Press
2 Police Square Milnthorpe Cumbria LA7 7PY
Tel: 015395 62069 Fax: 015395 63417
info@cicerone.co.uk www.cicerone.co.uk

CICERONE